THE ART OF SOULMAKING

FOR THE INCARCERATED

A PATH TO UNCONDITIONAL FREEDOM

Nicole Daedone
with Beth Wareham

soulmaker | PRESS

soulmaker | PRESS

soulmakerpress.com

Copyright © 2023 Soulmaker Press

All rights reserved. No part of this book may be reproduced in any form without written permission from the publisher.

ISBN: 978-1-961064-12-6

A priest stepped inside a dark cell; an incarcerated woman stepped forward to meet him. Nothing about this place or this person bothered him; in fact, he felt peaceful and at home. He extended his hands and said simply, "I am like you and I live in a place like this. Each day I have a rigid schedule. I am completely isolated from others and without the distractions of the world. Our experience has only one real difference: Choice. I chose the monastic life to transform myself and you were placed apart for punishment. Why not take my experience and make it your own?"

The priest then proposed to the incarcerated woman that she see her life inside in a new way. This prison, he suggested, is the monastery, a place of change and growth. Everyone is here for a reason, he went on, and it's not the reason most believe it to be.

"You, your friends, the correctional officers, the staff," he said, "were all brought together to transform. This is no accident. You were called here, and it has nothing to do with guilt or innocence, crime or punishment. This is the monastery; this is the gift."

She laughed and he smiled; he knew. Though concrete and fencing restricted her space to feet and inches, nothing prevented her from traveling inside herself and exploring a vast new world with no beginning and no end.

CONTENTS

Starting Your Journey

Letters to The Newcomer 1

How to Get the Most from this Course 5

The Art of Soulmaking Syllabus 7

Genius Is Your Calling 13

Welcome to *The Art of Soulmaking* 17

The Soulmaker Movement: Principles 25

Spirit Versus Soul 31

Assessments and Questionnaires 33

Practice

One Acre of Land 39

How to Work Your Acre: Introduction to Morning Practice 41

Lessons

Lesson 1: The Hidden Master 61

Lesson 2: Get Back to Where You Once Belonged 69

Lesson 3: Every Voice Inside of You Is Trying to Help You 81

Lesson 4: You Were Chosen For Forgiveness 91

The Journey Continues

Commitments & How to Support You 97
Post-Program Assessment and Questionnaire 99

WAYS TO STAY INVOLVED
Share Your Experience 109
Writing Release Form 111
Soulmaking Community 113
Soulmaking Group Facilitator Application 115

Additional Letters to the Newcomer 117
From the Authors. 121

LETTERS TO THE NEWCOMER

In the following pages you will find two letters from individuals who've studied and followed *The Art of Soulmaking* (AoS) program. One is written by a man who served thirty-three years on death row before being executed in the February of 2023. The other, by a woman who is a retired pastor. Both were eager to provide advice for the newcomer who encounters this path. Two additional letters are included in the back of this book.

Letter to The Art of Soulmaking *Newcomer:*

We all want to be free. Whether we dwell in a prison cell block or live in a luxurious home, there is a longing for the freedom from our innermost fears. Freedom from the internal voice that says "I'm unworthy" and fills us with unhealthy guilt and shame. It's also the source of our self-destructive patterns, whether they be self-doubts or the feeling of hopelessness. The prisons we build inside us are way more restrictive than any prison made of concrete, bars, and barbed wire could ever be. I know this because like you, I, too have dwelled in both.

This program offers us a way of breaking out of our inner prisons and finding self-liberation. Many of the ideas may seem a little bizarre, but if you take the time to study and put what's written into practice, you might be surprised with the outcome. What is there to lose for giving it a go?

Some of the things you will learn are self-compassion, and how to view your past in a better light. You will learn how to embrace all aspects of your personal makeup which will give you more strength and a sense of completeness.

This is not a program that's going to judge you, nor is it going to tell you what you should or are supposed to do. Instead, it offers simple yet effective ways for you to discover the inner freedom that's possible regardless of what your circumstance or situation might be. It doesn't matter who you are or what you may have done, unconditional freedom is yours for the having. So, are you willing to take this opportunity and discover new possibilities you never thought possible before? Inner freedom is yours.

BRIGHTEST BLESSINGS
Donald Dillbeck

Donald was incarcerated at the age of fifteen, and was executed in 2023, after thirty-three years imprisoned in the State of Florida. Donald was an active participant, mentor, and advocate for *The Art of Soulmaking* program.

To the Newcomers, Welcome!

I'm writing as someone who has found participating in The Art of Soulmaking *to be life-giving and transformative. I hope you will, too.*

I began about a year ago as a volunteer pen pal writing to prisoners. I'm an old woman (in my late seventies) and a retired pastor who just moved to a new state. I've been on a spiritual path most of my life, and have appreciated many traditions, as well as those who seek to know themselves and find their own truths. I love AoS's basic principles, especially that we engage as equals.

I learn so much from my pen pals. Often, I have found I am confronted with a different interpretation of ideas I've held for a long time. The chance to reappraise, and to enlarge my perspective, or to revisit personal issues, is sometimes uncomfortable but always valuable.

It is a privilege to share another's journey, and I find inspiration in doing so.

The program invites us to learn more about ourselves, and it gives us useful tools. Some come naturally to me, some not—I have to do yoga daily because my aging body hurts if I don't, but meditation I confess to doing irregularly. However, every time I return to sit, I'm glad I did. Not because I'm "good at it," but because it settles me down.

I usually find Soul Letters to be very powerful. As I sit down to write I am reminded of a very old spiritual tradition of going on a pilgrimage to some sacred place. These pilgrims often walked for many weeks; most were poor and slept in the rough. (Don't think high-tech hiking gear or a comfy car and nice motels.) Most people set out seeking a miracle—such as healing, relief from pain, forgiveness, or a reunion with a lost loved one. But the 'miracles' granted were often the personal growth and understanding gained along the way, rather than the changes originally hoped for. This is what we all really gain in our journeys with The Art of Soulmaking: *understanding how we can flourish in our current circumstances however difficult they may be.*

May each of you find blessings of Companionship and Peace on your journey.

Anne

A retired Episcopal priest and psychotherapist, Anne is a volunteer letter writer with *The Art of Soulmaking* program.

HOW TO GET THE MOST FROM THIS COURSE

Here are a few tips on how to get the most from this course and graduate from the program.

All participants who complete the syllabus are eligible to graduate with a Certificate of Completion. Where possible, we work with county, state and federal parole boards to educate them on what it means to be an *Art of Soulmaking* graduate, so that you can use this certificate to demonstrate your time well spent.

Before you start, we ask that you read the syllabus on the following pages. It's broken down into eight weeks of studying the workbook and includes assignments to help you integrate the content.

Your first assignment is to fill out both the human flourishing pre-assessment and pre-program questionnaire, and submit them to us electronically or by mail. One of your final assignments upon completing the course is to fill out both the human flourishing post-assessment and post-program questionnaire and do the same. This will help us measure how effective this course was for you and in doing so, help us bring this coursework to more incarcerated people.

As you complete your assignments, we'd love to hear about anything else that may be coming up for you. We have a team of people who have all been through this course and want to help guide others like you through it. We promise to reply to every letter you send us, and in our reply we will include a pre-stamped envelope for you to write us back. We want to hear about your experiences, what you are learning, how your life is changing, what you may be struggling with. And we will share with you ours.

We encourage you, wherever possible, to share this course with a friend. Read the book together. Ask each other the lesson prompts at the end of each chapter. Meditate or practice yoga together. Share your Soul Letters. Get to know one another in this way.

Even better, if you can, do this course with a partner, or in a group.

Our aim here is not only to heal pain, but to alchemize it. We want to teach you how to put that pain to use, converting it into meaning and purpose.

It is often at our lowest, we are given the opportunity for this conversion. We take everything that is stuck deep inside of ourselves — every emotion, every memory, every heartbreak, every choice we regret — and we use it. The point is not to fix what's down there, it's to use what's down there to change the world.

At the end of your journey we'll offer two more opportunities for ways you can extend your Soulmaking journey — you can contribute a personal story about your experiences and participate in The Soulmaking Community Groups.

Finally, it is okay to take your time. We understand that some of this material is difficult. We designed the syllabus to go at a steady pace, giving you enough time to sink into your daily practices and thoughtfully complete the integration exercises.

We look forward to hearing from you.

THE ART OF SOULMAKING
SYLLABUS

This 8-week curriculum will ensure you get the most out of this program. All of the below assignments must be completed to receive your graduation certificate. We are here if you need support or additional time to complete the program—do not hesitate to reach out.

WEEK 1

Introduction to the program, orientation to the Soulmaker Movement and our mission

Assignments

i. Read pages 1-38 of your workbook

ii. Complete the human flourishing pre-assessment and pre-program questionnaire

iii. Write a letter introducing yourself and what called you to this program

iv. Submit your assessment, questionnaire, and introduction letter

WEEK 2

We suggest daily practices because that's the best way to build a habit, but don't be discouraged if you find you miss a day or two. As with any new skill, it's hardest at the beginning, and the days you may not want to show up for your practices are likely the ones you need them most. Have compassion and kindness towards yourself as you embark on this journey of practices.

Assignments

i. Read pages 39-59 of your workbook
ii. 20 minutes of yoga daily
iii. 20 minutes of writing on whichever Soul Letter prompt speaks to you that day
iv. 10 minutes of meditation daily
v. Submit a letter about how practices are going and what you're noticing

WEEK 3

Completion of Lesson 1

Assignments

i. Read pages 60-67 of your workbook
ii. 20 minutes of yoga daily
iii. 20 minutes of writing on whichever Soul Letter prompt speaks to you that day
iv. 10 minutes of meditation daily
v. Write out your responses to Lesson 1 Integration Exercises
vi. Submit your integration exercise responses and an update about your practices

WEEK 4

Completion of Lesson 2

Assignments

    i. Read pages 68-79 of your workbook

    ii. 20 minutes of yoga daily

    iii. 20 minutes of writing on whichever Soul Letter prompt speaks to you that day

    iv. 15 minutes of meditation daily

    v. Write out your responses to Lesson 2 Integration Exercises

    vi. Submit your integration exercise responses and an update about your practices

WEEK 5

Completion of Lesson 3

Assignments

    i. Read pages 80-89 of your workbook

    ii. 20 minutes of yoga daily

    iii. 20 minutes of writing on whichever Soul Letter prompt speaks to you that day

    iv. 15 minutes of meditation daily

    v. Write out your responses to Lesson 3 Integration Exercises

    vi. Submit your integration exercise responses and an update about your practices

WEEK 6

Completion of Lesson 4

Assignments

    i.   Read pages 90-96 of your workbook

    ii. 20 minutes of yoga daily

    iii. 20 minutes of writing on whichever Soul Letter prompt speaks to you that day

    iv. 20 minutes of meditation daily

    v.   Write out your responses to Lesson 4 Integration Exercises

    vi. Submit your integration exercise responses and an update about your practices

WEEK 7

Commitments

Assignments

    i.   Read pages 97-109 of your workbook

    ii. 20 minutes of yoga daily

    iii. 20 minutes of writing on whichever Soul Letter prompt speaks to you that day

    iv. 20 minutes of meditation daily

    v.   Write out your responses to Commitments and How to Support You exercises

    vi. Complete the human flourishing post-assessment and post-program questionnaire

    vii. Submit your Commitment/Support exercise responses, assessment, questionnaire and an update about your practices

WEEK 8

Graduation

Assignments

    i. Read pages 111-116 of your workbook

    ii. 20 minutes of yoga daily

    iii. 20 minutes of writing on whichever Soul Letter prompt speaks to you that day

    iv. 20 minutes of meditation daily

    v. Write to confirm that you received your Certificate of Completion, whether or not you plan to write a story about your experience with this program, and include your application if you'd like to become a Soulmaking Facilitator

GENIUS IS YOUR CALLING

We tend to think of a genius as a person who solves the world's most complex math problems or writes beautiful songs. But genius is a force; not a person. One person can demonstrate the force of genius in one moment, and not in the other. Albert Einstein had non-genius moments. It's a force that passes through us, just as is love, or compassion. We prepare our bodies, and soften our minds, to open them to access genius. And then we wait. We do not own it; it does not belong to us, and it is our birthright.

A poet described the experience well. She was in the fields of her family farm working one day when she felt an almost imperceptible shift in the air. Her mind and body prepared for what was coming. She knew the feeling well; a poem was barreling toward her over the rolling green. All she had to do was run inside, write it down and begin refining it.

Genius is the mediating energy that takes the raw materials — in this case, words whispered over the soybeans to a poet-farmer — and transforms the energy into an object of beauty or something of use. Genius directs the purpose and aim of our existence; it's the energy that drives us to create, express, move, beget, forgive and invent.

When you work with the mediating energy of genius to create something beautiful or useful or true, you become crazy-wise, drawing upon everything inside your interior castle. Rational thought does not have the upper hand here; crazy-wise draws upon impulse, whispers, seemingly random memory and emotions flaring like spots on the sun. Your genius uses crazy-wise as its

"I think everything in life is art. What you do. How you dress. The way you love someone, and how you talk. Your smile and your personality. What you believe in, and all your dreams. The way you drink your tea. How you decorate your home. Or party. Your grocery list. The food you make. How your writing looks. And the way you feel. Life is art."

~HELENA BONHAM CARTER

fuel as you create. In your creation, you break the rules instead of letting the rules break your body and your life.

For centuries, human beings have used a retreat experience for self-reflection in order to contribute to a larger society. Removed from worldly pursuits and problems, the experience of incarceration becomes an opportunity for self-reflection, meditation and transformation. This is fertile ground for the force of genius to enter and instill this sense of purpose, to heal themselves, and society.

Imagine a younger you, 12 or 13 years old, growing up in the neighborhood you grew up in, attending the school you attended. Exposed to the same temptations you grew up in. Then imagine you have the option. A sober, transformed community member, who has done the work of clearing their heart of hatred, who is a contributing member of society, offers to mentor you. Or, there is a professionally trained therapist, fresh out of school, loaded with grand theories of psychology and the mechanics of how the human mind works. They offer unlimited theory to explain the pains and anxieties the younger you feels. Who do you want as your mentor?

Consider Caravaggio, a violent, easily offended man who lived more than 500 years ago and heard the call to paint. He was in and out of jail constantly for various troubles and, fleeing his home after an attempted murder charge, he continued to paint on the run. He painted Bible scenes, but his genius spoke differently than other painters of the day. His holy subjects were depicted with gritty realism not unlike the inside of a prison or a dark alleyway; light rakes across the figures as if streaming in through a small high opening. His models were people he met on the street. Death of the Virgin used a drowned prostitute as the figure of Mary and when the painting arrived at the Vatican, a scandalized Pope returned it.

Caravaggio's genius was the ability to draw in all his experience, all the darkness he'd seen and felt, and transform it with paint, no matter his circumstance. His life was often chaos, full of poverty and rage, but his canvases were carefully planned out. Why was this seemingly "crazy man" driven to such expression? His scenes were not "pretty;" they were powerful, heartbreaking, and heartfelt. His genius gave dignity to the silent lives of millions; in Caravaggio's eyes, a saint could resemble a common man. He converted anger, pain, isolation, and impulse into visions that now hang in the great churches and museums of the world. And no matter where he was or how fast he was running, he painted. He accepted what he was and where he was and he fully engaged with his calling. Caravaggio instinctively used alchemy, changing pain into beauty. He connected deeply with his genius and changed the course of Western art.

What Is Your Genius?

When we listen for the genius that lives inside us, we also bring out the wisdom of our community, of the people around us. When we look after what is beautiful inside of us, we bring out the beauty in others. Have you ever noticed that when you take a little more care of your appearance, suddenly everything around you seems to brighten in your presence? This same beautification works for your interior world, too. Heal yourself within and watch those around you transform. Soften your heart, soften your mind, allow yourself to see love around you, even in the midst of great injustice and harm, and you will notice the people around you begin to soften, too.

Reception is like a cellphone picking up a signal. The stronger the signal, the more clearly we hear the caller on the other end. Suddenly where it was just a vague buzz with the indistinct words, you can hear the voice. Is it angry, is it sad, are they proud of themselves, are they happier than usual? But this clarity starts from within. We get to determine how many bars of reception we have.

As we increase our reception, we find more resources. Resources can be fifty bucks in your pocket, but it can also be that day when you have a little more patience, where you don't get upset with the person who usually annoys you even though they are doing the same dumb thing they do every day. This is how we wake up the genius within. We answer the call inside of us. We pick up the phone call from our soul. Then we don't need to yell at anyone else. Our beaming bright signal will draw them back home to themselves.

A Caution as You Enter this Path

Please be aware what we are offering to you is a difficult path. You can continue in old ways, disavowing yourself by claiming superior spiritual ideals and praying desperately that wild forces inside of you do not reappear. This path asks you to name your pain and grief and rage, examine them and become friends. On those terms, these feelings become your power — fierce, loyal, *meeked*.

In *Spirituality and Psychological Health*, Dr. Steven Diamond writes:

> Spirituality, secular or religious, is a serious enterprise with potentially perilous consequences. For all who dare venture into the true 'spiritual' realm — the passionate, shadowy domain of the daimons — must be psychologically and emotionally prepared to meet the metaphorical dark deities, forces, powers or spirits, abandoning all hope, as Dante forewarned, of finding only friendly, benign or benevolent ones. Many seekers, alas, are not. Herein lies a common recipe for spiritual disaster...
>
> In the final analysis, the fundamental task of a secular spiritual psychology is to redeem (rather than cast out or exorcise) our devils and demons. It is inevitably both a psychological and spiritual venture. Psychotherapy such as this is one way of coming to terms with the daemonic. By bravely voicing our inner "demons" — symbolizing those unconscious tendencies we most fear, flee from, and hence, are obsessed or haunted by — we transmute them into helpful spiritual allies, in the form of newly liberated, life-giving psychic energy, for use in constructive activity. During this process, the strange paradox that many artists and spiritual savants embrace is discovered: that same devil so righteously run from and rejected turns out to be the redemptive source of vitality, creativity and authentic spirituality. (Stephen Diamond, "Psychotherapy, Evil, and the Daimonic: Toward a Secular Spiritual Psychology," in *Spirituality and Psychological Health*.)

WELCOME TO
THE ART OF SOULMAKING

This program seeks to repurpose the experience of incarceration from mere punishment to something truly restorative that transforms the individual from harmful to uncovering their unique purpose and contribution to society. The goal of this transformation is to benefit both the individual and society, and the prison experience is turned into one that is beneficial. Welcome to this journey.

We have all heard "the meek shall inherit the earth;" and we all have ideas of what the "meek" look like: weak, forgotten, taken advantage of.

Putting this phrase in the context in which it was written; over 2,000 years ago, in a language other than English, the phrase takes on a different meaning. The ancient Greek word for meek, "praus" (πραεῖς), was used to refer to a horse trained for battle. Wild stallions were captured for riding, pulling and general labor. For these horses, it was essential that their wild nature be broken, so that they could work efficiently and not threaten the required monotony of their work. Of those horses, there were a set who, despite the best training, always retained a part of that wild nature. These horses were trained, disciplined and obedient, but never broken. Society learned that these horses were underutilized as domesticated horses. Instead, they found a far more productive use for them; these were the horses they used for battle. They kept the best qualities of their wild nature; their fierceness, their raw power, while also developing a willingness to be disciplined and responsive. They'd fearlessly gallop directly into battle, but they'd come to a sliding stop at the nudge of their rider's leg. Their power was their willingness to be disciplined, despite not having to be. They chose it. These horses were the most valuable horses in the land.

You, like us, have been invited to enter a new life in the same way as the wild horse. The calling of this path is not to break your spirit, but rather to be "meeked." To retain your wild nature, while building the necessary discipline so that that nature can be put toward good use.

The world of the soul is different from the world of the spirit. Spirit is light, orderly, clear, and rational. Spirit lives in the mind. There is stillness. Soul is dark, wild, creative, alive, and nonrational. Soul embraces all aspects of life including things that seem dirty or broken. Soul lives in the body. If we have one without the other, we are half-realized, imbalanced. Ideally, we stay down in the soul and spirit floods in. Spirit and soul merge in union in the body. We are able to cycle between the light and the dark. They balance each other.

Letting go is something desperately feared by this light world. Control and presenting well are the highest currency. This light world can get fixated on achievement, material or spiritual, and status. If you are incarcerated, you exist as a warning about what happens if one does "let go;" if they were to honor any bit of that wild nature that exists inside every one of us, they may wind up where you are. Those who are incarcerated bear the greatest punishment that exists, which is isolation, because they carry the scary shadow of those who want to let go.

A bit more about what we mean by shadow. Shadow is a psychological term, which means a repressed or unacknowledged characteristic. The light is easy to see; the shadow is more elusive. Take, for example, two women who are long-time friends. One arrives at the other's house with a new handbag and necklace. Her friend immediately notices and says, "Who gave you THAT?"

An argument takes place between the friends that is nothing more than one woman projecting her feelings of envy and lack of worth on the other.

Why wasn't one friend happy for the other's new things? Why does it matter to her? She won't admit that she's envious; she can't. She can only express her situation as superiority and ridicule. She can't express envy because she literally can't "see it," she can't acknowledge it. At least not yet. It's in her shadow, the part of herself unknown to herself. This woman with the new handbag and necklace represents her own repressed desire to have something nice for herself.

People experiencing incarceration, who exist at the fringes of society, who have experienced breaking the rules, their wild nature expressed even in the face of undesired consequences, represent the shadow of every human being. We all want to let go, we just want to let go safely. Many in society don't believe they can do it safely so they never let go. They look at your situation in prison as the picture of what it would mean to let go, and they don't like what they see.

In this way, your position as the holder of the shadow of society is one of nobility. You, at the "bottom," are free to look up and see the exposed underbelly of society. You can see its judgments, its contractions, its hypocrisy, its pain, in ways others on top cannot. You can see its shadow in ways it cannot. This is the privilege of your position.

PART ONE of your initiation is to choose to accept your position — to receive the hatred, the projections of inferiority, the accusations and disdain. Your initiation is to take it and to not take it personally. Soul gives the toughest battles to the strongest soldiers. **PART TWO** is to forgive; to release your claim to repayment for what has happened to you, and the resentment for any hurt caused to you during this journey to where you are now. You are to clear your heart of hatred and blame, and send this poison you have taken in back out as love.

We have a friend, a pen pal on death row. We chose to write to him because of all the letters we read, his letters demonstrated that he had eyes to see. Every other letter, and we read thousands, contained the sentence, "I am not supposed to be here."

We understand what you go through is a process, much like wailing over the dead is a part of grief. This is to be expected. But your guilt or innocence is of no interest to us; it is a straw man who breaks apart with the slightest breeze. What matters is, what are you going to do with this experience right now? It is the same question wherever you are; can you see a higher power in the center of the experience? If you are not guilty, take every legal step to get out. But for present purposes, you are here now. What will you make of this life?

The person we chose was the one who said, "I am here." He communicated a profound acceptance. In initiation, the answer to every prayer is acceptance; acceptance is freedom rather than giving in.

He told a story of how in the prison he was in, everyone suggested that he become a Christian because Christians were more likely to get time off their sentences and enjoyed liberties that other residents didn't. It was a well-known scam. He may be incarcerated, he said, but he could not pretend to be something he was not. He had not, in fact, ever heard or felt God. It would have been a lie to say he had.

Then, one night as he was laying in his bunk in his cell, he felt a presence. He did hear a voice. And clear as day, the voice told him that he could be free right where he was if he would help others right where he was. He feared that he had nothing to offer but was "told" that if he just said yes, he would be given the power. He said yes. He could not say if it was Jesus or any particular form of God, only he knew in his bones that what he heard was real. That he could trust.

He simply started looking for where others were in need. He'd listen to the guy whose wife decided that she couldn't take his being in prison and was filing for divorce. He listened to the guy who got a cancer diagnosis and was going to die in prison.

He showed up for the guy who got the crap kicked out of him. He was no expert, he just showed up. He released his blame towards the correctional officers and slowly, very slowly, built a rapport of civility. He understood they, too, were answering their call and executing it at times with grace, at times with cruelty, but that his work was to answer to the judge within his heart.

The next thing he knew, guys were lining up to talk to him. He didn't know how, but he knew the right thing to say. Something inside him woke up, a kind of knowing that went beyond him. One day he realized that he was totally free, right where he was. He realized he was freer than he ever was on the outside and freer than anyone he'd ever met. He was granted a peace beyond human understanding. He realized that wherever he was, if his body were to be set free tomorrow, he would simply continue to do the same thing. So he stopped fighting.

He realized that he was posted to this station because he "could" be. He had what it took, a conviction about who he was, an unwillingness to pretend, an honesty. And that this made him the perfect candidate to be the master of this particular location (although he might not have called himself such).

This man taught us much about the workings of life that cannot be learned from the great texts or in protected "safe" environments. He had in-the-field training and an experiential compassion that felt otherworldly. Corresponding with him, you had the intuitive sense that he would flinch at nothing we could share with him. There was no aspect of our lives, our beliefs, that he would reject. Not because he was so high, so distanced from it, but because of the profound depth of acceptance that he carved out in his own life and extended to everyone he met.

Because he was so "low," he had lived through worse than most people around him had, he had room to receive them. His was a most intimate compassion. This is what the realization of the soul looks like — where you go from theoretical ideas of what being "good" means, to actual experiences of it.

You face the horrors of your own mind: Can you remain conscious here? Can you hold true to the values in your heart here? Under the most heinous duress? When everything in you is reduced to survival, to self-preservation, when you are being treated like an animal — can you offer yourself there? In these dark environments are the last test and proof of one's conviction where there is no room for lofty ideas.

He realized that wherever he was, if his body were to be set free tomorrow, he would still be the same man he was right then, in his cell.

Like our pen pal friend, you came in as wild as the ancient Greek "praus." You can deny your situation, fight it and make it wrong. You have free will. But this will not do what this initiation is here to do and that is to free your soul. From any condition whatsoever. And in the process, become one, who by your very existence, frees others.

From here, I cannot describe the beauty of the world that emerges. To have nothing but truth move you. To see all the nakedness of emperors. To be granted x-ray vision. To be able to love as much as the human heart wants to. Even the correctional officers and the wardens of the world. To welcome them all.

This course is about the journey into the inner-workings of your soul; Soul*making*. Unconditional freedom is that field. There is no right and wrong here, no political conservatives against black activists, no Left, no Right, no camps, no correctional officers. Here, you are free.

We recognize the very things you believe are wrong with you — your history, your failings, your mental health issues, your obsessions, your fanaticism and your mania, your fear and your loneliness, pre-qualify you.

A person in prison meditates in a cell that becomes an inner monastery for transformation; a musician hiding from soldiers re-imagines the sound of gunshots into a guitar solo; a painter paints her own horrific accident again and again; a mother writes in her kitchen, alone, long into the night; an architect builds a cathedral over a slave pit; a composer turns weeping into a song. Magicians all, they seek their truth no matter the constraints of society's boundaries and laws. Their craft of taking the very pain

---

"Out beyond ideas of wrongdoing and rightdoing there is a field. I'll meet you there. When the soul lies down in that grass the world is too full to talk about."

~RUMI

in front of them and transforming this pain into an offering to society transforms them in the process.

A word we'll use throughout this course to describe this process is alchemy. We've all heard of this before in our culture. "Making lemonade from lemons." "Turning lead into gold." In soulmaking, you use alchemy for your soul. Think of the victim who forgives her aggressor and the two create a theatre show about forgiveness, reaching thousands with their message. The husband and wife who lose a biological child and decide to adopt two more who'd otherwise grow up in orphanages.

We invite you to become the alchemist of your own experiences, your own heart. Your obstacles, setbacks, heartbreaks and loss become pure gold: pain transforms into something beautiful, something that connects us to one another, something of use to society. You become crazy-wise, converting all that has touched you into a non-rational approach of soul, and applying it, with rigor, to the practical rational world of science, consciousness practices and social change.

THE SOULMAKER MOVEMENT: PRINCIPLES

Reunion: Wholeness Requires the Individual

We believe the work of the individual is to know the whole of creation. To do so, we orient ourselves around the truth and seek to harmonize the deepest expression of our unique blueprint with the whole of creation. When we bind ourselves to the inward image of our soul—to our blueprint—and fully express who we essentially are, that expression will draw us into ever-deepening intimacy with our environment, with nature, with others around us. We know ourselves by knowing the world, and we know the world by knowing ourselves; in doing so, we unite heaven and earth, below and above, within and without.

Alchemy: Convert the Smog of the World into Oxygen

Our work is to draw in the war of the world, the pain, and radiate it back out as love. Because we no longer see ourselves as separate from the world, we relate to the pain and the war of the world as an externalized reflection of our inward state. So, we purify ourselves by loving that which our conditioning would see as distasteful in the world. The alchemical process of individuation requires us to direct our attention to light up within. By doing this, we transform 'lead' into 'gold' and from there, we can covert the smog of the world into oxygen.

Circulation: Fill What Is Empty and Empty What Is Full

Our focus and path are love, and our means is circulation. A healthy heart keeps energy circulating throughout the body and in the world. In alchemy, this is referred to as the *circulatio*, in which the material is repeatedly dissolved, sublimated, and coagulated. We fill what is empty and empty what is full.

Co-creation: The Bee and the Flower Are Equally Benefitting
We recognize the mutuality of existence as connected beings and do the work to develop the capacity to both transmit and receive energy. The bee transmits pollen and receives nectar. In the process, the bee gets sustenance and the flower gets to reproduce; both are equally receiving. All persons are caught in an inescapable network of mutuality, tied into a single garment of destiny. Whatever affects one directly, affects all indirectly. As in: 'I can never be what I ought to be until you are what you ought to be, and you can never be what you ought to be until I am what I ought to be.' Co-creation is a reciprocal process where everyone benefits. Together, we build an entire ecology. We are all in this together.

Meeked-ness: The Meeked Shall Inherit the Earth
We believe the meeked shall inherit the earth. The ancient Greek word for meek, "praus" ($πραεῖς$), was used to refer to a horse trained for battle. Wild stallions were captured for riding, pulling, and general labor. For these horses, it was essential that their wild nature be broken. Of those horses, there was a set that, despite the best training, always retained a part of that wild nature. These horses were trained, disciplined, and obedient, but never broken. They were unconditional. The stallion that is the 'meeked' one, retained his wild nature and is the most obedient to the unalterable truth. Meekedness is reserved for the strongest among us. For when the strongest are obedient to unalterable truth, they can endure the weight of compassion and open-heartedness.

Remembrance: Remember to Remember
We believe we already know. Our only work is to remember. And then to remember to remember. When the situation is the most challenging, we remember to remember. We leave reminders at the door of consciousness to get back to our bodies and retain

the beginner's mind over and over. To 'remember to remember' is to remember to seek *anamnesis*—to remember to go inward and recover what we've always already known.

Incarnation: Build the New that Makes the Old Obsolete
We believe the purpose of life is not to ascend, but to incarnate—to draw heaven down to earth. As such, we must become good stewards of our inheritance. To do this, we evoke our heirloom humanity through the process of re-wilding. We allow our nature to take over, heal itself, and grow freely. That is how we turn corn back into maize. Our task is to remember the wisdom of our soul and reshape the world through the expression of that wisdom. We came here to infuse the material world with spirit, to incandesce the world. From here, we build the new that makes the old obsolete.

Cultivation: Bring Forth What Is within You (Gospel of St. Thomas)
Our journey is to become the artist who can bring forth the truths of the human soul with exquisite beauty. "If you bring forth what is within you, what you bring forth will save you. If you do not bring forth what is within you, what you do not bring forth will destroy you." There is union between spirit and soul. We meet in that location. We welcome the daimon that is equal parts destruction and creation and believe that which is not integrated is exaggerated.

Play: Potential Is Discovered in Play
We believe potential is realized in play. In the words of Maslow, we've focused enough on the ailment. It is time to focus on the potential; that is what we aim to do through converting the "negative" stagnation into potential and using it according to each person's desire. We find this while in a state of play. The world and all its trauma is not a hell-realm to be overcome but a playground to be made love to. To seek freedom in all conditions is to drop ourselves into uncomfortable positions and see how we can infuse those conditions with levity, spontaneity, and play and

allow ourselves be surprised by our own creative responses and resourcefulness. By changing the stakes, the one who plays allows for possibility, uncovers hidden talents, and lives in their genius.

Purposefulness: Your Pain Is Your Purpose
Our pain is our purpose. To harvest the fruits of our pain, it is not enough to merely heal. It is our unique calling, our path. Our pain thus becomes the path to our greatness. We turn poison into medicine.

Rehumanizing: We Are Inestimably Powerful
We believe in the inestimable power of each and begin each conversation, both personal and cultural, as such. We do not need to find 'Oz' in order have brains, heart, and courage. We merely need to remind ourselves the power is already inside of us. We are already home. Those who society has marginalized—the imprisoned, the mentally ill, the homeless, the crazy ones—have the most unexplored potential. The only option is to learn how to work with them in such a way as to turn lead into gold and see what the 'wild ones' may have to teach us. We believe that in 're-humanizing' the marginalized, we unlock the power of the world.

Unconditionality: Freedom in All Conditions
We aim for the unconditional—love, Eros, freedom, and truth without exception. We believe each of us must be trained in unconditional freedom; how to find meaning and purpose right where we are. This creates resilient, kind, present, resourceful, playful human beings. We approve of all conditions, both internal and external, that create barriers to full expression. Obstacles are the path—freedom beyond circumstance, in all conditions.

Eudaimonia: **Unique Blueprint Leads to Human Flourishing**
We believe in the notion of *eudaimonia*, that within each of us is a unique blueprint or calling that when expressed, leads us to a state of flourishing. This in turn brings the precise, vital nutrient the world is missing. Einstein said, "If you judge a fish by its ability to climb a tree, it will always look stupid." We believe in judging

each person by the metrics of their arena. To use generalized measurements of 'value' and 'worth' to people robs them from developing and expressing their uniqueness, and leaves us with a culture lacking what genius would contribute.

Synthesis: Genius Is Found in Synthesis
Eros is the union of opposites into a bigger whole. Genius is found in synthesis, the marriage of opposites. We recognize the space that separates can connect. The unions of light and dark, good and bad, rational and nonrational, open up a third path. This marriage between the letter of the law and spirit of the law gives birth to a higher truth.

Pacify: Emanate a Spirit of Peace to a Turbulent World
We believe in re-instating flow when circulation is constricted. To pacify is to send in Eros—the unifying spirit when someone feels agitated or out of alignment. Emanate a pacifying energy; radiate it. We trust that holding our own interiors calm in an increasingly shaken world is the maker of harmony.

Collective: The Next Leader Will Be the Collective
We believe it will be the collective that will transform the world. When we as a community inhabit the spirit of Eros, the community itself becomes the leader. From here, we serve the numinous instead of the numinous serving us.

Reception: True Power Is that of Reception
True power, like gravity, is the power of reception. It converts the repugnant into the desirable. What if we were the answer to the question of our time, Will you receive me? Will you receive me unconditionally, without judgment or agenda? We believe in the taking in of the whole world, the way one would make love to the whole of the world.

Our Mission

Our mission is to transform hearts and open minds. In doing so, we seek to convert a judgmental, closed society into a community of open, conscious individuals who place the ultimate value on creativity, truth, connection, and love. We seek unconditional freedom where the self is never chained, no matter the outward circumstances.

Our method uses the examined interior life to effect change on the exterior. Heal thyself and heal the world; connect to thyself and connect to the world; free thyself, free the world; serve thyself by serving the world.

Why We Do What We Do

Our experience is that life is purposeful. Purposeful in that we are all here to make our unique contribution to society. There is living "in your life," and there is living "out of your life." Either can happen anywhere and at any time.

"Living in your life" is living with a purpose. You are emotionally available, and you exist in an interchange with the people around you, where you are enriched by your environment, just as your environment enriches you. Life is deepening over time. "Living out of your life" looks like denial, self-consciousness, distraction, and refusing to digest the emotional content of your life. "In" is heaven; "out" is hell. "In" can happen in a prison cell just as easily as "out" can happen in a cathedral. Your environment does not dictate your life.

True healing in the world will arise not from the completion of a battle of ideas, but rather from a group of people who agree to live *in* their life.

SPIRIT VERSUS SOUL

A brief overview of John Tarrant's seminal *The Light Inside the Dark* (1998) divides our consciousness into "spirit" and "soul," opposing poles that work in tandem to make a whole human being.

"Spirit" is transparent, and it is given. It cannot be produced by focusing on it; one must grow quiet and uncover it. It is our tie to a vast eternity, a stillness where there is no content. Spirit is where you were born, and where you shall return. Connecting to it requires a practice: meditation, prayer, and the long, slow process of letting go that drops us into a place where the still center comes into view. When we make contact with it, we understand there is no beginning and no end. We are what came before, and we are what will come again.

Spirit is the purview of religions, where the rules are clear and ordered. With spirit, our life here is clearly seen and shines down in all directions. Yet alone, spirit is weak, too clear about its goals, reckless and headlong in its pursuit of them. Spirit is too full of absolutes. Alone, it cannot engage with the unpredictable, delicious, heartbreaking joy known as life.

At the other pole is "soul," a dirty-faced, beaming actor full of sound and fury, gasping and laughter. Soul bubbles up from below where the wildness lives; it is always trying to embrace things, inhabiting the brokenness of the world. Soul is creative: it produces something out of matter. It's how we connect with others and feel less lonely in tangible human ways.

Soul loves to live and learn; it is always trying to embrace things. It brings meaning to experience, including the thoughtful aspects of our being. It throws its arms around what we know most dimly of ourselves or sometimes shudder at: hidden passions and insomnia; helpless, almost indestructible longings, obsession, ruminations, and secrets; and the continuing undercurrent of knowledge that some losses are irretrievable. Soul is the gift that makes us less perfect, so that we can be more whole.

Having one without the other creates a misshapen interior. Without the positive and negative charges of soul and spirit, consciousness, like molecules, falls to pieces. By moving between the two—a cycling between the white light of spirit and the darker earthier depths of soul—the organism is brought back into balance. We are complete. If spirit is too dominant, long-repressed natural appetites become swollen and explode with tragic consequences. Soul left to its own devices is a Bugatti racer with no brakes.

Employed together, a pleasing tension arises between spirit and soul. Rational thought and wild creativity flourish in the same organism quite peacefully.

If spirit is represented by light and lives in the mind, soul emanates from the body and is charged with a wild eroticism that drives creation. Put them together, and learn what it feels to be complete.

ASSESSMENTS AND QUESTIONNAIRES

The Human Flourishing Assessment is used to measure people's overall fulfillment level. At the start of your journey, you will complete the Human Flourishing Pre-Assessment. Once you complete the program, you will complete the Human Flourishing Post-Assessment.

The Program Questionnaire asks about your emotions, thoughts, and actions. You will fill out this questionnaire at the start and end of the course so you can see if there were any changes in your emotions, thoughts, and actions.

The Human Flourishing Pre-Assessment and the Pre-Program Questionnaire are part of what you will mail or email back with your week one assignment. The Human Flourishing Post-Program Assessment and the Post-Program Questionnaire are part of what you will mail or email back with your week seven assignment.

HUMAN FLOURISHING PRE-ASSESSMENT

Name:

Select your level of agreement with each statement
(*only choose one answer*)

1. In general, I feel confident and positive about myself.

   STRONGLY AGREE   AGREE   UNDECIDED

   DISAGREE   STRONGLY DISAGREE

2. I made some mistakes in the past, but I feel that all in all everything has worked out for the best.

   STRONGLY AGREE   AGREE   UNDECIDED

   DISAGREE   STRONGLY DISAGREE

3. Many days I wake up feeling discouraged about how I have lived my life.

   STRONGLY AGREE   AGREE   UNDECIDED

   DISAGREE   STRONGLY DISAGREE

4. My relationships are as satisfying as I would want them to be.

   STRONGLY AGREE   AGREE   UNDECIDED

   DISAGREE   STRONGLY DISAGREE

5. I believe I have discovered who I really am.

   STRONGLY AGREE   AGREE   UNDECIDED

   DISAGREE   STRONGLY DISAGREE

6. **My life is centered around a set of core beliefs that give meaning to my life.**

   STRONGLY AGREE   AGREE   UNDECIDED

   DISAGREE   STRONGLY DISAGREE

7. **I can say that I have found my purpose in life.**

   STRONGLY AGREE   AGREE   UNDECIDED

   DISAGREE   STRONGLY DISAGREE

8. **I believe I know what I was meant to do in life.**

   STRONGLY AGREE   AGREE   UNDECIDED

   DISAGREE   STRONGLY DISAGREE

9. **I have confidence in my opinions, even if they are contrary to the general consensus.**

   STRONGLY AGREE   AGREE   UNDECIDED

   DISAGREE   STRONGLY DISAGREE

10. **I usually know what I should do because some actions just feel right to me.**

    STRONGLY AGREE   AGREE   UNDECIDED

    DISAGREE   STRONGLY DISAGREE

11. **I find I get intensely involved in many of the things I do each day.**

    STRONGLY AGREE   AGREE   UNDECIDED

    DISAGREE   STRONGLY DISAGREE

12. **I feel best when I'm doing something worth investing a great deal of effort in.**

    STRONGLY AGREE   AGREE   UNDECIDED

    DISAGREE   STRONGLY DISAGREE

13. **When I engage in activities that involve my best potentials, I have this sense of really being alive.**

    STRONGLY AGREE   AGREE   UNDECIDED

    DISAGREE   STRONGLY DISAGREE

PRE-PROGRAM QUESTIONNAIRE

Name:

Select your level of agreement with each statement
(*only choose one answer*)

1. **On a scale of 1-10,** (1 being the lowest and 10 being the highest) **please circle below how much stress you feel on a day-to-day basis?**

    1   2   3   4   5   6   7   8   9   10

2. **On a scale of 1-10,** (1 being the lowest and 10 being the highest) **please circle below how angry you feel on a day-to-day basis?**

    1   2   3   4   5   6   7   8   9   10

3. **On a scale of 1-10,** (1 being the lowest and 10 being the highest) **please circle below how optimistic you are about your life?**

    1   2   3   4   5   6   7   8   9   10

4. **On a scale of 1-10,** (1 being the lowest and 10 being the highest) **how significant a role do drugs, alcohol, or other substances play in your life?**

    1   2   3   4   5   6   7   8   9   10

5. **How frequently do you get into physical fights?**
   (Please circle your answer below.)

    NEVER   INFREQUENTLY   SOMETIMES

        SOMEWHAT OFTEN   OFTEN

6. **How frequently do you get into verbal fights?**
   (Please circle your answer below.)

   NEVER　　　INFREQUENTLY　　　SOMETIMES

   SOMEWHAT OFTEN　　　OFTEN

7. **Do you ever feel depressed?** (Please circle your answer below.)

   NEVER　　　INFREQUENTLY　　　SOMETIMES

   SOMEWHAT OFTEN　　　OFTEN

8. **Do you ever have suicidal thoughts?** (Please circle your answer below.)

   NEVER　　　INFREQUENTLY　　　SOMETIMES

   SOMEWHAT OFTEN　　　OFTEN

9. **How often do you feel grateful for your life?**
   (Please circle your answer below.)

   NEVER　　　INFREQUENTLY　　　SOMETIMES

   SOMEWHAT OFTEN　　　OFTEN

ONE ACRE OF LAND

To paraphrase writer Anne Lamott, imagine that every newborn is given an acre of land. That acre represents what they will grow and nurture in this life; except this acre is your soul. You can grow what you love; tomatoes, watermelon, spinach and apples, or you can allow weeds to choke out the body-building foods, leaving you nothing but bitter leaves and poisonous berries.

There's a gate on one side of your acre; you get to choose who gets inside and who must stay out; that is a huge part of life. Who are you letting inside? Once in, what do they do? Are they creators or destroyers? This choice is as important as the plants you put in your dirt.

Tend your acre with great care. Touch the soil with your hands. Is it hydrated, and well-tilled? Does it feel dry, deserted? Either way, this is your plot. You only have one. Value, self-satisfaction and purpose all grow from this acre. In the end, that's what you cultivate.

HOW TO WORK YOUR ACRE

Introduction to Morning Practice

Morning Practice is your daily tending to your soil. This is your base; everything grows from here. The care and attention you put inside determines what comes out of you.

Morning Practice can be enjoyable at times, something you look forward to. Other days, it may seem like a drag. This is no different than any other kind of mastery; they all involve dedication. Monks sit in meditation daily, no matter their mood. NBA players practice countless layups and pivots before they take it outside. Both will tell you, the less you want to do it, the more you need to do. They practice their genius relentlessly. They bring to practice their problems, frustrations, pain. Their practice becomes a sacred space that is only theirs, where slowly they begin to trust.

Practice is about disrupting autopilot. This precious time opens you to receive the deeper truths often masked by your own negative thought loops, intense emotions and/or other people's comments. You will come to look forward to the repetitive nature, the ritual of your morning and receiving its fresh energy and new insights into you and your life.

In this section, you will find instructions for yoga, your Daily Soul Letters, and seated meditation. The yoga postures, or asanas, help invigorate your body and provide energy for the day. Writing Daily Soul Letters helps you get to know yourself on a deeper level, as you will often discover things you did not expect.

Life is a practice. To gain skill at anything, you must do it and then do it again, over and over, to gain confidence and mastery. The more skillful you become, the more life you live. Commit to this practice just as you would a fitness regime because that's what it is, a workout to strengthen your soul.

"The nature of yoga is to shine the light of awareness into the darkest corners of the body."

~JASON CRANDELL

Meditation reduces stress, develops concentration and opens you to connect with your own deeper wisdom and creativity.

Each practice can stand alone, but we strongly recommend that you commit to at least one hour per day. Here is a possible structure:
1. **20 minutes of yoga**
2. **20 minutes of writing Daily Soul Letters**
3. **20 minutes of seated meditation**

Yoga

The main thing about yoga is to remember to listen to your body above all else. If something is painful, ease up. If something feels great and you want to go deeper, feel free. The body often opens when we relax and constricts when we push.

One round of Sun Salutations is a series of twelve yoga poses that flow together in coordination with the breath. Their purpose is to warm up the body at the beginning of yoga class before practicing individual poses. Beginning students typically take 10 minutes to do three rounds of Sun Salutations, which leaves 10 minutes for relaxation at the end. The final relaxation is as important as the Sun Salutations. After you have learned this basic series, we'll offer more variations in later courses. Most importantly, have fun!

To start, come to a comfortable, cross-legged seated position. Place a pillow or a rolled up blanket or sweatshirt underneath your hips. This way the hips are higher than the ankles and you can sit more comfortably. Roll your pelvis slightly forward so you can ground down through the front of your sitz bones — the ones you sit on at the base of your pelvis. Hands can rest comfortably on the knees, shoulders relaxed, chin parallel to the floor. Close the eyes and take a couple of deep breaths here. Typical yoga breathing is in through the nose and out through the nose. As you breathe deeply into the abdomen, let the belly expand. Then as you exhale, draw the belly button in toward your spine. Many of us breathe the opposite of this pattern, so don't worry if it takes some practice to get it.

Start standing with feet parallel, hip width's distance apart. Knees above ankles. Hips above knees. Shoulders above hips. Rock back and forth till you find your center from front to back. Shift your weight side to side until you find your weight equally distributed between right and left. Roll your shoulders back and down. Hands by your sides. Palms can be facing forward. Chin parallel to the ground. Imagine someone is pulling a string out of the crown of your head, lengthening your spine.

1. Inhale. Then as you exhale, bring your palms together in front of your chest.

2. Inhale extend your arms out front and move them up alongside the ears, palms facing each other. Take a gentle backward bend from just beneath the shoulders.

3. Exhale hinging forward into the **Standing Forward Fold** with a flat back releasing and relaxing over the legs. Let the spine lengthen and the head hang. You can nod the head yes, shake the head no, relaxing and releasing all the muscles in the back of the neck. Place your hands on either side of the feet, fingertips in line with the toe tips. Bend your knees, if you need to, to get the palms flat on the floor.

4. Inhale. Stretch the left leg far back and come into **Low Lunge**. Left knee comes down to the floor. Release the top of the left foot on the floor. Make sure the right knee stays directly above the right ankle. Your front shin is perpendicular to the floor. If the knee goes past the front ankle, it can put too much stress on the knee joint. You can come up onto the fingertips. Lengthen out the back of the neck. Drop the pelvis down and stretch. (If you have any knee pain, place a blanket or pillow underneath that back knee.)

5. Exhale to move into **Downward Facing Dog** (**Down Dog** for short). If you have a four-legged friend, you've probably seen them do this! Weight is distributed evenly between hands and feet. If you want to, take a few breaths here. You can alternate bending one knee and stretching the arch of that foot and then straightening it when you bend the other knee and stretch the opposite arch. Do this a few times. Bring your chest closer to the floor. Keep ears in between upper arms. Bend your knees and tilt the sitz bones — those are the ones you sit on at the base of your pelvis — up toward the sky. If at any point Down Dog becomes too intense, you can: 1) put your forearms and elbows down on the ground instead of just your hands, or 2) come down and

rest in **Child's Pose** (not pictured). To rest in Child's Pose, drop your knees, shins and tops of the feet down to the floor and sit back on your heels with your arms stretching out in front of you. Your forehead rests on the ground. (Come back to Down Dog to transition into the next pose.)

6. Bring knees down to the floor, then chest down, then chin down. Keep the pelvis slightly raised and toes tucked under. Elbows are in close to the sides of the body.

7. Press through the toes and slide the torso along the floor until the legs are straight. Inhale to come into **Baby Cobra**. Release the tops of the feet onto the floor. There is no weight in the palms. The head, neck and chest are slightly lifting off the ground. Bring your awareness to your upper back. Imagine the shoulder blades are sliding down your back toward the base of your spine. Elbows stay in close to the body. Back of the neck is long. Look up with the eyes.

8. Tuck the toes, press into the palms, lift the hips, and exhale into **Down Dog**.

9. Inhale. Bring left foot forward in between the hands to come into **Low Lunge** on the left side. Let the right knee rest on the floor. (Again, if you have any knee pain, place a blanket or pillow underneath that back knee.) Make sure the left knee stays directly above the left ankle. Drop your pelvis down while you lengthen your spine.

10. Exhale. Bring the right foot forward to meet the left and come into the **Standing Forward Fold**. Release and relax the head and the neck. Imagine that your head is heavy like a bowling ball and completely let it go.

11. Inhale. Bring your arms up alongside your head. Hinge up with a flat back. Bend your knees, if you need to, to protect your lower back. Take a gentle backward bend at the top of the inhalation from just beneath the shoulders.

12. Exhale. Palms together in front of the heart. Congratulations! You just completed your first round of Sun Salutations!

Now release the hands to the sides. Feet remain hip distance apart. Close the eyes and observe the effects of your first round of Sun Salutations. Your heart might be beating slightly faster than before, your breath might have changed in some way or you may feel a bit warmer. You may not notice anything at all. And that's okay, too!

Repeat the Sun Salutation series (poses 1-12) two more times.

With practice, you will get the movement and breath pattern down and start to feel your own flow. Yoga is different from exercise. It is consciously moving with your breath and becoming aware of how you feel in each moment. Three rounds of Sun Salutations take about ten minutes and are a great way to start the day.

Most importantly, after you finish all three rounds of Sun Salutations, lie down on your back for **Final Relaxation**. Feet are about 2-3 feet apart. Palms are facing up and about a foot away from the sides of the body. Set a timer for ten minutes, close the eyes and relax here. This lets the body integrate the benefits from the Sun Salutations.

Modification: If you have any lower back pain, bend your knees up and place your feet flat on the floor. Separate your feet wider than your hips and let your knees rest against each other. Close the eyes. You can do the **Final Relaxation Pose** with your knees bent.

Daily Soul Letters

Once your body is open and warm from the yoga, take out a pad of paper and spend twenty minutes writing. Nothing is off limits; this letter is for you and you alone.

Writing Daily Soul Letters is your soul's cannon; you are writing a doctrine on the way your soul wants to express. This is the place where you begin to meet yourself and this is a conversation, one which will continue your entire life. This is you speaking to your soul, and your soul speaking back to you. This is not about receiving guidance from High Above; this is about sinking in, speaking to the small, still animal inside of you.

Guide the writing and let the writing guide you; this is what your soul wants to express. Like prayer, soulmaking is a conversation and, as one Rabbi put it, "In prayer, God is a verb." Like all communication, if one speaks and no one is listening, it's not communication; it's noise. The connection between two or more, the golden thread that connects us all, of speaking and listening, listening and speaking, cannot be broken.

Other verbs such as loving, sharing, dancing and hugging are the same. Without the golden thread connecting two humans, the action — as well as the verb that describes it — no longer exists. There is no hug, no love, no God without the verb.

All of life is a verb because of the need to connect our thread to another soul. In this way, prayer becomes God-ing. In human relationships, one person is wife-ing while the other is husband-ing. We are all verbs, Joan-ing and Mark-ing our way through the world, connected and in need of one another. As you Joan and Mark, you learn through the connection that we are all the same thing.

When Mother Teresa prayed, she spoke and she listened. As you develop in your soulmaking, you'll sit down to write and ideas, emotions and memories will come to you, seemingly from nowhere. Write it all down and as your inner castle forms, shapes become clearer. Each morning, when you take up your writing, you meet your soul again in a never-ending conversation. As your journey goes deeper, you can revisit your younger "soulmaking self" and feel how far you've come... as well as how far you'd like to go.

Your one acre of land, your soul, the very dirt that makes you who you are, is turned over and aerated each day as you write your inventory. In this way, you see, and more importantly, feel yourself, your energy, your desires, your dreams. You can care for the abandoned spaces within yourself and release what no longer serves you. In this way, day by day, we make the soul and move toward unconditional freedom, no matter the circumstances in which we may find ourselves.

"If it'll keep my heart soft, break my heart every day."

~WARSAN SHIRE

"God speaks in the silence of the heart, and we listen. And then we speak to God from the fullness of our heart and God listens. And this listening and this speaking is what prayer is meant to be."

~MOTHER TERESA

THE WAY IT IS
There's a thread you follow. It goes among things that change. But it doesn't change. People wonder about what you are pursuing. You have to explain about the thread. But it is hard for others to see. While you hold it you can't get lost. Tragedies happen; people get hurt or die; and you suffer and get old. Nothing you do can stop time's unfolding. You don't ever let go of the thread.

~WILLIAM STAFFORD

Below are different soul exercises that will help you mine the gold inside, your genius, your soul. Use some and not others; once again, this is about choice and what is most effective for you.

Sit down and start with this simple question: what wants to be heard and what wants to be said?

Dreams

A dream can be tricky, but the key is to pay attention to the different types of dreams you have. Some have messages, lessons, memories, premonitions, themes or abstractions, and others may be a random expression of your subconscious. The more you pay attention, the more interesting you will find them. If you relive a certain memory, note it and how it may change in your mind as you dream it. Repetitive dreams of falling often represent fear; dreams of forgetting to wear clothes can represent insecurity. If you have a feeling upon waking, note that as well.

Automatic Writing

According to Aletheia Luna, automatic writing is "the practice of writing words in a trance-like state that originates from outside conscious awareness." She explains, "Psychologists and spiritualists have varying beliefs about the origin of automatic writing, with some arguing that it is sourced from the unconscious mind, and others claiming that it originates from supernatural forces such as spirit guides and angels."

Sit comfortably with your pen and paper. You can have open eyes or close them; whichever helps you focus. Some days, stories will push up through your pen as will thoughts and feelings you may or may not know you ever had. Ask a question of the Universe or ask for help. If this doesn't work for you the first time you try, try it again. Practice requires repetition if you are to receive its true benefits.

"The whole purpose of automatic writing is to access guidance from your Soul, especially if you struggle to hear it in daily life."

~ALETHEIA LUNA

Body sensations (tingles, heat, relaxation)

Sensations in the body reflect your psyche's needs. Because your body contains many memories and secrets — both "good" and uncomfortable ones — feelings in the body are meant to alert you to the deeper state of your being. It may seem that body pain and pleasure are circumstantial experiences, which don't tell us much. That's a limited view of the body and its relationship to the soul. In truth, your body's feelings often reflect your psyche's needs. Awareness about your body is a wake-up call to regain contact with the inner self and reach beyond self-consciousness toward seamless immersion in the purpose of your life.

Say you're reading a book you love; there is no space between you and the story. When you are focused on it, the world falls away and you are at one with the experience. That's what you aim for, being in the zone, and living in a state where your insides match your outsides. You want to be where the story and the reader become one.

When do you last remember having no sense of time? Perhaps you were involved in a story or a conversation. Perhaps you were writing or drawing. Write about what feels timeless to you.

Community Reflection (Loving Tree)

Sometimes it's hard to see ourselves clearly, so it helps to surround ourselves with people we trust who can remind us of who we really are or help translate/interpret our experiences when we are bogged down and can't see the way.

The Himba tribe of southern Africa has a unique method of reminding tribe members of who they are: they sing the person's song back to them.

The Himba are one of the few people who count the birthdate of a child not from the day they are born or conceived but the day the mother decides to have the child. When she decides, she goes off and sits under a tree, by herself, and listens until she can hear the song of the child who wants to come. And after she's heard the song of this child, she comes back to the man who will be the child's father and teaches him the song. When they make love to physically conceive the child, they sing the song of the child as a way of inviting him/her into the world.

When she becomes pregnant, the mother teaches that child's song to the midwives and the old women of the village, so that when the child is born, the old women and the family gather around the child and sing their song to welcome them. As the child grows up, other villagers are taught the child's song. If the child falls, or gets hurt, someone picks them up and sings them their song. When the child does something wonderful or passes through the rites of puberty, the people of the village honor the child by singing their song.

One other occasion calls for the "child's song" to be sung. If a tribesman or tribeswoman commits a crime or something that is against the Himba social norms, the villagers call them into the center of the village and the community forms a circle around them. Then they sing their birth song to them.

The Himba view this moment as a correction, not as a punishment, but as love and remembrance of identity. For when you recognize your own song, you have no desire or need to do anything that would hurt another. In marriage, the songs of the man and the woman are sung together. And finally, when the Himba tribesman/tribeswoman is lying in their bed, ready to die, all the villagers who know their song come and sing — for the last time, that person's song.

Do you have a song? What is it? How does it tell us who you are? Does your friend have a song? What is it? Have you ever sung each other's song by way of greeting? Try it.

Stress

"Feeling stressed" is a catch-all term that means nothing except you cannot express how and what you feel; it's all a wall of anger and exhaustion. Your soul is on lockdown and you feel almost nothing but a free-floating unsourced anger.

"Stress is the gift that alerts you to your asleepness. Feelings like anger or sadness exist only to alert you to the fact that you're believing your own stories."

~BYRON KATIE

Your physical being is screaming at you and if you don't listen, injury to your body, mind and spirit will result. One of the reasons for Morning Practice is it creates a sense of relaxation and peace to start your day; it is like money in the bank for when stress comes.

If you feel "stressed," what exactly are the feelings?

What do you believe to be the underlying reason? Write about it.

Writing and Drawing

Writing and drawing are essential tools in exploring your own soul; you dive down and let what comes come, then you'll rise refreshed, rejuvenated and renewed. Renowned psychiatrist Carl Jung asked his patients to make their own books, drawing and journaling and scribbling down ideas and random thoughts. He encouraged them to make their own archetypes; one's mother could be The Destroyer or The Rescuer while a father can be The Punisher or The Runner.

In this way, they told of their soul's passage, or *nekyia*, through the psychic underworld, in a therapeutic practice that neutralized negative thoughts and traumatic memories.

Visions During Meditation

Meditating is a powerful way to experience what has been referred to as the mystical experience. One common mystical experience involves tuning into visions or spontaneous names while you're meditating. During meditation, an entire scene drops into your mind, seemingly out of nowhere, or you might hear words or names. These visions or names might be of your current spirit guide or messages from your soul.

Mystical experiences are so powerful, they have changed the course of human history. They unleash creative energies and often provide solutions effortlessly to some of life's greatest challenges. They are without end. The more you meditate, the more you have.

A master of meditation says, "Let me sit with it." And he or she means just that. By simply being still and clearing the mind,

> *"I should advise you to put it all down as beautifully as you can. It will seem as if you were making the visions banal — but then you need to do that — then you are freed from the power of them... Then when these things are in some precious book you can go to the book and turn over the pages and for you it will be your church — your cathedral — the silent places of your spirit where you will find renewal. If anyone tells you that it is morbid or neurotic and you listen to them — then you will lose your soul — for in that book is your soul."*
>
> ~ANALYSIS NOTEBOOKS,
> C. G. JUNG QUOTED IN
> THE RED BOOK, *LIBER NOVUS*

you invite a miraculous world in. When you "sit with it," what do you hear and see?

Desire

Desires are your soul speaking to you, telling you what it wants. You may crave intimacy or chocolate cake. Desires in and of themselves are beyond "good" and "bad": they just are. Accepting you have them is not the same as acting upon them, and only you know what is "good" or "bad" for your soul.

It's your acre of land, remember?

Do you feel a specific desire(s)? Write about it/them.

Meditation

As far as we know, meditation has been practiced for at least two thousand, five hundred years. Why? As great a gift as it is to be able to think as human beings do, thinking alone cannot make a person whole. In truth, thinking often gets in the way of knowing our whole selves. And at worst thinking can feel like sheer torture.

Sometimes, we need a break. This is the simplest reason to meditate.

But thinking is a natural process. No matter how hard you try, you can't just stop thinking.

It can't be willed away any more than you can will away breathing.

So we find another way. We learn to watch our thoughts rather than getting ourselves tangled up in them. As someone chooses to develop a practice of sitting quietly, breathing and watching her own thinking, when she is ready, a change will begin to occur. It may start slowly as her river of thoughts begins to slow. And then it may become clearer, that while you have been watching the mud and the rocks and debris wash by, you have been missing something else in the stream of thoughts, something that can

---

"Which we call libido, and whose nature it is to bring forth the useful and the harmful, the good and the bad."

~CARL JUNG; CW 5;
SYMBOLS OF TRANSFORMATION

"Meditation does not itself accomplish the tasks of life but provides spaciousness, bringing the great background near, so that whatever we do, rising in the quiet, has force and beauty. In meditation, we take time, sit down, watch, while the silence accumulates — which is how the spirit gathers to a vessel the soul has prepared."

~JOHN TARRANT

only be seen as the waters still, and it is glittering like gold at the bottom.

Ultimately meditation is for that, to help you see clearly and come to realize that the gold in the river is You.

Find a quiet place. If you can't find a quiet place, find the quietest place you can. If you have a way to track the time, that will be helpful.

There are two options for sitting.

One is on a chair with your feet flat on the floor.

The other is to get a pillow (or *zafu*) and find a place on the floor or a bed where you can sit cross-legged.

You will want to sit on the edge of the pillow, which may need folding in half for more height to allow for the slight natural curve at the base of your spine. This is what's called "a straight back." But everyone's body is different, so everyone has different needs for creating the right position to sit.

It takes a little experimenting.

If you're sitting on a chair, you may find that you need to sit forward a bit to get your feet flat on the ground and keep your back fairly straight. When seated either on a chair or the floor, tilt the top of your pelvis forward slightly. This allows you to ground down through the front of the sitz bones — named for the bones you actually sit on when you sit in proper alignment.

If you're sitting cross-legged on a blanket you might need to put some extra cushioning like a sweatshirt or towel under each knee. Sitting cross-legged, you may think of your knees and pelvis as creating a triangular base above which the spine can balance. But you'll find out for yourself what gives you the greatest stability and ease as a position.

So now you're sitting.

These are some questions you might want to ask yourself. You're looking for what's really happening with your body, not what you think should be happening. And if you can't maintain the sitting up posture for long, don't worry about it. Move to a more comfortable position and come back to sitting more upright when you're ready.

You sit down all the time; what's the difference with this? To start with, instead of sitting down, you might try sitting up. But instead of making a command of yourself, try making a request. Can I grow taller inside myself? (What does that feel like?) Can I draw air into my body more easily when I sit up this way? Or that? Does my spine feel more supportive when it's in alignment with my head and my hips?

Once you're sitting, you probably want to close your eyes so you won't be distracted by what's outside you. Now turn your attention to your breathing. You don't have to do anything about it, just watch what it's doing. Is it fast? Slow? Ragged? Smooth? Can you watch your breath without trying to change it in any way at all? It may change itself but see if you can watch for that to happen. Or not.

This is the soft wild animal of yourself you're watching, and she's doing what she does all the time quite well, without your attention. But pay attention now. Keep watching your breaths.

Thinking often stands in the way of quieting the mind, criticizing or judging how and what you're doing. And it's okay. Thinking is okay. But in this practice, thinking is not the boss.

So to keep the thinking part of yourself occupied, you might want to try counting your breaths – from one to ten. That's all. You reach ten and start over at one. Sometimes this is enough to satisfy your thinking mind. Sometimes you'll find it wanders off somewhere else and you lose track of the breaths you were counting. That's fine. Just start over at one. You can always go back to one. All you want to do is to keep sitting.

You may find it relaxing. You may find it dull as dirt. However you find it now, just know that it will change. And try not to forget that thinking itself doesn't want to be quieted. Thinking will want to get back to its usual chatter and position of calling all the shots. (It really doesn't always know what's good for it.) But if you make a firm decision to keep sitting, no matter what your thoughts seem to say, you may find at some point that you've learned to grow taller and quieter inside. And just that is a relief.

Start with ten minutes. Eyes closed. Watching your breath. Ten minutes is often enough time to start with. Within ten minutes you may begin to sense that your mind is like one of those little snow globes, and as you sit, it will be like watching the snow settle to the floor. That's great.

When the ten minutes becomes easier, you can increase your sitting to fifteen minutes. Notice the difference in your mind and body doing that. And when that becomes comfortable, try sitting

Try to sit for ten minutes at first. This is a good place to begin meditating.

twenty minutes. Don't skip straight to fifteen or twenty minutes to start. Take your time. You want to notice the differences along the way.

Practice is key, but the opportunities for finding authentic freedom inside increase as you come to rest in more and more moments of deepening quiet.

There is more to this, but this is where it begins.

The gold is inside—here, in you.

"Recall my words to you here and now and reflect on them when you feel that old habit or that pang of insecurity that's nagging in the back of your mind saying, 'You know they're right, you are not good enough, you are not pretty enough.' All you've got to do is look in your heart of hearts, and feel how your heart beats; it beats to your soul's drum. It's not a skin color, it's not a race that has it beating so fiercely, it's your essence."

~Willie, Texas Dept. of Criminal Justice, Ferguson Unit

THE HIDDEN MASTER

LESSON 1

Start with the challenging idea that you are perfect and were perfectly created for love. This lesson flows through every other lesson in the soulmaker's progress. You may feel uncomfortable at first because of other programming you've received. Let's melt through that and get to love.

Basic Goodness

The mind is a powerful warden. The body, our soul, our refuge and salvation, can often seem difficult to enter. Some have left themselves so long ago, they forgot that home is within.

Looking for your own self-worth from the outside world, energy and talents are aimed at continuing to elicit someone, or something, to say yes, you are good. You live in a state of sinking, hopping from inflated life raft to life raft as people affirm to you your value. You have grown accustomed to hanging onto these rafts, to hearing the air slowly escape and the dark water slowly pulling you down. This is what we consider hell; living locked out of ourselves.

This pattern continues. If it is not a good deed, it is the right job. You will be happy when you find the right job. It is the perfect partner, the perfect family. Everything; anything but you.

A woman sits in her prison cell. She looks at her clothes; she did not choose these clothes.

She looks at her room; small, shared, with a heavy steel door. The door reminds her that it opens not on her command, but on others'. The door reminds her that her family, her friends, may never walk into this room she is in now. This is hers alone to navigate. She walks to the cafeteria to eat; she did not pick this meal. Everywhere she looks, she sees messages that she is not to be trusted with choice because of what she did.

When you've lost track of your innate goodness, everything you experience gets measured up against, "Does this make me

> *"The first guy I met in prison told me I could sit in my cell and slowly stagnate and go insane like the vast majority of the people in solitary OR I could turn my cell into a monastery and continue to grow, evolve, and learn."*
>
> ~DAMIEN ECHOLS, ACTOR, PRODUCER AND FORMER DEATH ROW INMATE

good or does this make me bad?" This is why we grasp at success and drown in failure. When we strive for that brief "pleasing" and "winning" feeling at the cost of inner peace and a clean conscience. Who are you pleasing? What do you win?"

In the hardest of times, how do you remember that what is inside of you is made of Good? When everywhere you look you are reminded of hurt, and the reminder of hurt instills a sense of shame. The shame has that hurt pierce through, "I did something wrong," and you begin to believe, "I am something wrong."

Facing what seems like insurmountable challenges, you may have already given up the idea of your life having value or ever even being able to enjoy it. You might even feel you live beyond redemption; you feel the cause of "you" is lost.

We weren't born with self-hatred. Recount a time you felt value. It probably involved other people, it probably involved you feeling in some way connected to something greater than yourself — a family, a community of friends, a school, co-workers, a sense of purpose. The feeling of self-worth was tied to your sense of being connected and of belonging to something other than yourself. At once you felt both fulfilled personally and that you had a place. This is not an idea, or something you gain. It's a human experience to which we all have a claim.

There is this place. Beyond, there is a field, where right and wrong do not exist. This is where we ask you to meet us. There is a beauty indescribable when you break through the belief that you must earn your way. There is such a thing as real wealth; and that is wealth of the soul. It is a wealth that says you do not live paycheck to paycheck of your last good deed, or of the last person who smiled at you and acknowledged you as a human. This wealth is something you were endowed with when you came onto this earth. It is not a wealth you earn; it is a wealth you remember. We are here to walk you home.

This is all to say, value is not a man-made concept. An innocent place lives inside you and it never changes no matter what; it's a quality that no one can take away, not even you. Receiving and

---

"The Shamans say that being a medicine man begins by falling into the power of the demons; The one who pulls out of the dark place becomes the medicine man, and the one who stays in it is the sick person."

~JOAN HALIFAX, AMERICAN ZEN BUDDHIST TEACHER

giving love exists in every heart beating beneath every ribcage; there's nothing you could do or say to change that.

After you accept your basic goodness, you will still feel pain. Life continues to go on, on life's terms. But you do approach the pain differently. You'll shift away from running from it and come to see it as the sign that more awakening is near. The sting doesn't lessen; but the experience of the sting changes with this new sense of purpose to it. Your experience of pain becomes a part of your path toward your genius, your higher purpose.

Whatever your injuries, this course is about shifting your mind so you begin to see problems and difficult emotions in your life as opportunities to deepen your experience of your life; to carve out more of the emotional scar tissue. Stop performing for others and work on building a relationship with yourself and your Higher Power, your Creator, your God.

God as You Understand God

You decide what God is for you. You decide what word you use, too. God, Spirit, Higher Power, Universe, Divine Order, Great Mystery. This course is secular; we use the term God, for simplicity. You get to define God for yourself just as you get to write the story of your own life.

Soulmaking requires you believe that something greater than you decides your worth, your value; that you're here because you're supposed to be here. In soulmaking, the moment you decide you don't have worth or do have worth is a Godless moment; you do not have the power to make that call. God decides, and God believes in you.

It's not about solving the problems that the world, or your mind, present. That's just another version of you *doing* better, you twisting yourself in knots and jumping for the approval of others. Your sense of self-worth is about shifting your consciousness entirely, to one rooted in your basic goodness. Then you offer yourself to the situations you experience instead of needing "to get something" from them.

Once you've touched this freedom and flexibility in your mind, nothing else will do. There's an old saying that... "Once you've had one taste of the divine, nothing else will do and you will do anything to get it." You've exited the enslavement of proving yourself to others. You can inhale deep into your belly, long, slow breaths. You can savor air, you can savor your body nourishing from your breath. The simple becomes profound.

We believe that, for reasons only God understands, prison is a part of your spiritual path. We are here to teach you how to get "into" your life, how to get you rooted so deeply into the reality of your present experience, you are able to sink below or rise above the daily "fight" of life and tap into a new way of living centered in the heart. In this new way, your focus remains to find the presence of love everywhere, even while incarcerated. We believe this is what God intends for all of us.

The first step is to choose to suspend disbelief, in the name of discovering and experiencing this new way. The choice is to suspend fighting your current circumstances in order to settle into your present life, and yourself, to find out why you are here. We assert that by looking within yourself, you will always only see good because that's what's there.

Integration Exercises

Each day of this first week, after you've finished your Morning Practice, take a question below and write your answer. Take as much time and space as you desire.

Your Beliefs

- Do I have faith? How has my faith figured into living in a prison?

LESSON 1: THE HIDDEN MASTER

- What's something of value I offer to the people around me?

- Who do I love?

- Who loves me?

- Who do I trust? Why do I trust them?

- What is the meaning of my life?

Seeking Approval from Others

- What limiting beliefs remain in me that say I am bad or weak?

- In what ways do I look to people outside of myself for approval, rather than having courage to share my life experience?

- When have I allowed others to speak negatively about me and not stood up?

- Where did I accommodate cultural norms and pretend that I could or would change?

- Where did I bow to public opinion and betray the deeper meaning of my life?

Giving In to Shame-Based Fear

- When and how have I avoided working through my own doubts?

- Where did I hold myself to a lower standard than I deserved?

- Where have I used my skills for personal gain and not given back?

"I don't really like to call any feelings or states solely 'good' or 'bad.' To me, they are just like greed, delusion, jealousy, etc. I can't perceive them as 'good,' but they are opportunities to re-channel energy into something productive. This is what I'm trying to do with myself!"

~Diana Lovejoy, Central California Women's Facility

GET BACK TO WHERE YOU ONCE BELONGED

LESSON 2

Learn to convert pain's poison into the antidote: strength. By staying with uncomfortable or hurtful feelings, you burn out the negative energy, the charge. We'll show you how to do it so that you may let go of what does not serve you.

Defining the Challenge

Most people, whether in prison or on the outside, live inside a "cell." Theirs may not be made of metal, but they have locked their thoughts and emotions and very lives up, living as was once described, "in quiet desperation."

It is the woman with the perfect house, the perfect husband, and the perfect kids. She smiles as she walks through the grocery store, smiles as she passes her neighbors' home. She gets home and she is exhausted. She woke up not knowing she could make it through the day smiling, but she did. She doesn't know if she can tomorrow. Each day gets harder. Sometimes she notices how hard it is, other times, she's forgotten. Her husband, growing slightly distant, wants to reach her, but can't. He doesn't know how. He makes more money to remodel their house; he spends more time with the kids. She can't shake the unhappiness; the haunted feeling of another life she was meant to live. This is prison, too.

We don't mean to minimize your experience in prison, but we want you to understand the mechanics of what we call suffering. Suffering exists regardless of your circumstances. The physical place doesn't matter. Suffering is most characterized by the belief, "If I get ___, then I will be happy." It is the lack of presence in today's reality. More specifically, it is the refusal to accept today, until your demands are met. "I will be happy when I get out."

"What is required of us is that we love the difficult and learn to deal with it. In the difficult are the friendly forces, the hands that work on us. Right in the difficult we must have our joys, our happiness, our dreams: there against the depth of this background, they stand out, there for the first time we see how beautiful they are."

~RAINER MARIA RILKE,
GERMAN POET AND NOVELIST

"I will be happy when my husband comes back." "I will be happy when my health improves." This is suffering.

In order to hide from pain and not face feelings, people go to great lengths to avoid confronting this suffering. At its worst, they go dead inside, refusing to experience the dynamism and pleasure of being human. The only way to experience unconditional freedom — and we mean unconditional — is to look into the depth of your emotions and voices of your soul and to feel them. Acceptance is what sets you free.

Every human being experiences pain. It could be physical pain from accidents, injuries or abuse. Emotional pain from moments of being hurt or feeling rejected, abandoned or betrayed. Perhaps a sense of emotional guilt and shame snake through you, dark persistent feelings that you failed at life or let people down.

Few have the tools to actually deal with it. You can act out against it; reject it and live in exhausting denial, avoid and numb it with drugs or alcohol or junk food, or, worst of all, try to fix it, which is definitely above your pay grade in life. Only God "fixes" the world; you must stay in your body, closer to home.

This pain is moving as a ghost would move through your own life. At its worst, things feel empty, pointless, lacking; you cannot find meaning. You feel resigned to live this way; no hope of enjoyment, just an endless sense of going through the motions. In Far Eastern cultures like China, Vietnam and India, a Hungry Ghost is depicted as a spirit with a bloated stomach and a throat so narrow that eating is incredibly painful or impossible. It represents a hunger that cannot be fed, the lingering ghost of a tangible, satiable hunger. The Ghost can never be gratified by any amount of consumption. Think of the "Ghost" as the poor kid who could never be rich enough as an adult; a first generation American who never feels American enough; or an ex-lover wandering the world looking to recreate an old childhood dynamic; never able to meet someone as they are. Their stomachs will never fill.

People spend their entire lives hiding from pain. Then they find others who also hide, and they go on hiding from pain together. False personas meet false personas, but no real intimacy is ever created. They form common bonds as victims to other people or institutions. Think of the group of men who sit in a bar grumbling about their jobs, sharing with certainty their great complaints, but each individually never improving his life. They live with chronic complaints.

Or instead they bond around a common enemy, creating connection through complaint and counter-aggression. Or perhaps, they are the "nice ones," the ones there for support, shaking their heads at the carelessness of others. The group of the "nice ones" may feel commonality; but no one ever feels truly reached. No person gets to be truly known. Whole lives, families, and organizations are built in this way.

Harvesting is a term used for gathering food, from plants to fish and meat. You "harvest" vegetables from plants or shoot a deer in order to harvest its meat. In a larger sense, you can gather anything to add to your life, but if you cannot harvest your own pain, you will be buried by it. It will grow to define you. Pain and discomfort give you impulse to take action, but taking action distracts you from the real work of identifying and knowing the pain enough that it will reveal its secrets to you. Essentially our "doing," our endless busy-ness, chatter and diversions, keep us from our "being."

Drama Triangle

Our thoughts determine the quality of our life experience. Some of our thoughts have been with us since the beginning — many were inherited from our family members. These are our core beliefs, which could easily be called our unquestioned assumptions. "Unquestioned," yet we let them define us and our world. We let these beliefs create our story about who we are and what we can expect from the world.

Victimhood snakes through the consciousness of many, squeezing and squeezing the life out of them; victimhood feels more like the snake than anything Adam and Eve encountered. Its shape might surprise you. The head of this snake is fear, the fear

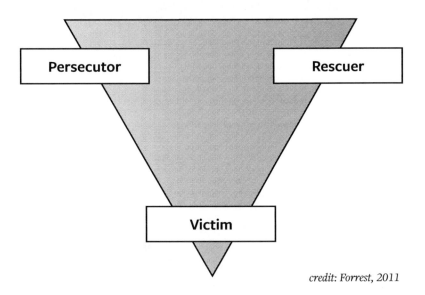

credit: Forrest, 2011

you will not survive either physically or mentally. The good news, and there is a little, is that being a victim implies that within you is a victor.

Being a victim also means you feel entitled — "I worked hard and that is my promotion;" "I was a great girlfriend and he left me;" "I do everything for my kids and they don't care one bit." You felt entitled to the job, the man and the love of your family and as soon as you embrace your role in the victimhood — the weight of your expectations set up the Victim Triangle — you begin to release yourself and move on.

As a victim, you can simmer with anger and plot revenge, but remember, there is no villain without you, the victim.

The original diagram (pictured above) was created by Dr. Stephen Karpman, and called the Drama Triangle. Author, Lynne Forrest, describes the three roles on the triangle as being primary defense strategies (victim/collapse, persecutor/attack and rescuer/fix) that we use to interact with one another and play out our own unhappy stories. Lynne refers to the Drama Triangle as the Victim Triangle, because we actually perpetuate victimhood using these three defense strategies. By feeling and reacting out of the unhappy thoughts and stories we blindly believe we hold ourselves captive in victim consciousness, and continue to go round and round on the Triangle.

Each position has its own particular way of seeing and reacting to the world. To help you better understand the three roles, we have included a story from each perspective: rescuer, persecutor and victim.

Rescuer

Jackie's mother was physically disabled and addicted to prescription drugs. From Jackie's earliest memory she reported feeling ultimately responsible for her mother. Instead of getting appropriate care from a parent who was concerned for her well-being, she became the "little parent" of a mother who played the part of a helpless child.

This childhood scenario set Jackie up with a "life script" that predisposed her towards becoming a rescuer. Care-taking others became her primary way of relating to people.

Rescuers, like Jackie, have an unconscious core belief that might go something like this, "My needs are not important… I am only valued for what I can do for others." Of course, believing these ideas requires her to have someone in her life who she can rescue (a victim). How else will someone like Jackie feel valuable and worthwhile?

Jackie would never admit to being a victim because in her mind, she is the one who must have the answers. Nonetheless, she does, in fact, rotate through the victim position on the triangle on a regular basis. A rescuer in the victim role becomes a martyr, complaining loudly, "After all I've done for you… this is the thanks I get!" (Forrest, 2011)

Persecutor

Bob is a doctor who often justified hurting others. Attack was his primary way of dealing with inconvenience, frustration or pain. Once, for instance, he mentioned running into a patient of his on the golf course. "Can you believe that patient had the nerve to ask me to treat his bad knee, right then and there, on my only day off?" Bob handled it by taking his patient to his office and "giving him a steroid shot he'll never forget!"

In other words, Bob rescued his inconsiderate patient, but in a way that "punished" him for daring to be so bold. To Bob, his action seemed rational, even justified. His patient had infringed on his free time, therefore, he believed, his patient deserved the rough treatment he got. This is a prime example of persecutor thinking. Bob didn't realize that he could have just said no to his patient's request for treatment. He did not have to feel victimized by it, nor did he need to rescue his patient. Setting boundaries never occurred to Bob as an option. In his mind he had been treated unjustly and therefore he had the right, even the obligation, to get even. (Forrest, 2011)

Victim

Janetta sees herself as consistently unable to handle life. She considers simple things like doing her laundry, cleaning the bathroom and preparing meals as overwhelming tasks. Constantly complaining of exhaustion, Janetta says to her partner, "You're the only one who can help me." She feels bad about herself and her inner dialogue is just plain mean. She thinks her own harsh critical voice just might be right about how incapable and incompetent she is after all.

You can enter the Victim Triangle from any point, but the movement and resolution you seek will never come as you drain your energy on this merry-go-round.

The Hardest Work Is to Stay with Yourself

Why do we hop onto the Victim Triangle? Because it is uncomfortable to sit in the sensation of our pain. We want to do something — drop it like it's hot, expel it from our bodies. It's fundamentally about not taking responsibility. Not in the way society chastises us for not taking responsibility, throwing out meaningless phrases like "you're lazy," or "you're lying." Remember, responsibility is not about what you do or don't do. It is about not taking responsibility for remembering your "beingness."

The temptation that follows this knee-jerk reaction, this desire to chatter, busy yourself and bolt from the challenge, is never about shiny objects outside of yourself. These restless feelings are about running from your own insides. Any place is more comfortable than there.

The avoidance patterns are endless. From victimhood, to perpetration, to denial, to compensation through achievement, drugs, food, our list of addictions go on. All of these methods end in the same result; continually diminishing results because the more you use them, the less they work. The more you use anger to cover up fear, the angrier you get. The more you use happiness to cover up pain, the happier you have to pretend to be.

The Antidote Is Made from the Venom

The very thing that there is so much of — pain — turns out to be the exact ingredient needed to transform your mind and your interior world from an unpredictable tumultuous roller coaster to something more like your own inner temple.

Pain is a lot like soil. Soil is made up of dirt and nutrients that enter the soil through decay — everything in life that has died or been released to the ground — somehow carries the nutrients that grow all plants, flowers, vegetables and fruits; everything that life is. Pain is to creativity as soil is to plants. Pain is the ground where creativity grows.

Say an addict gets sober and helps others get sober. She uses her very dark descent and terrible experiences to relate with and have other addicts know it's possible to have a new life. The pain — and the clear-eyed examination of it — resets and regenerates them all; their lives have meaning. Addiction has thus become a spiritual pathway; its pain and passion are redirected toward strength, healing and higher purpose.

When we have a solid footing of freedom within, it doesn't matter if you are being treated unfairly. Is your life really a mistake? Is this situation too much for you? In what way is it too much? You can spend a life avoiding pain and at the end of it, you will look back and find you have the same resentments you always did. They ran your life and now that life is ending.

We spend our lives avoiding the discomfort of pain, but facing it turns out to be the medicine that eases the discomfort. The antidote is made from the venom.

All that matters is, can you love even this? God sends us places and asks us to do the work. You happen to have received one of God's hardest assignments; but God reserves His hardest assignments for His toughest soldiers.

Integration Exercises

Questions to consider in your Daily Soul Letters practice:

- Where did I allow my victim archetype to take me hostage in a situation? What were the results?

- Where have I demanded that the world prove itself to me rather than me offering my support to the community?

- In what ways do I take care of people which I later grow to regret?

- Where did I, out of fear they'd leave me, render someone incapable?

- Where did I go too fast and not listen?

- What has God asked of me that I resent?

- What has God asked of me that I still have not done?

- What gifts have I received being in prison that I have refused to acknowledge?

- When and why did I choose to support people who did not contribute equally?

- Have I done the work to truly fortify my backbone?

"Pain comes with the human experience and avoiding it cheats us out of great lessons. Show me someone who has never experienced hardship or heartache. That person can't fathom depth. We come to realize how easy it is to not be caught up in the pain, to recognize it, to understand it, but not to attach to it."

~Donald Dillbeck, Union Correctional Institution, Florida

EVERY VOICE INSIDE OF YOU IS TRYING TO HELP YOU

LESSON 3

This lesson is more pain conversion work, as you learn to use alchemy to transmute difficult experiences into positive ones. In this way, you come to see that even what you perceive as "bad" is good.

How to Harvest Pain

Everything we experience carries a secret for us and it is our work in this world to find out what that secret is. Until we do, this experience will recur, over and over, until we can grow to receive it. Some of these experiences are positive. We will meet someone who reminds us of a loving friend who we were never able to be good to in return, and our second encounter grants us the opportunity to mend where we fell short the first time. In other cases, it's a negative experience. A loved one dies, followed shortly after by another. We are turned down on the spot from two job interviews, two days in a row.

These experiences carry with them their own emotional heaviness. For example, they incite in us joy, disgust, shame or grief. Each experience is its own initiation, its own entry point within. That is, a transition point for our soul. Your soul will attempt, again and again, to reconcile you with it. It is your bell, ringing over and over, to bring you home to you.

If God, or God however we understand God, intends for us to be naturally joyous and free, then it holds true that we can be joyous and free anywhere. Each experience is our opportunity to confront all the limitations of our mind which would otherwise have us not feel joy and freedom. This process is like a polishing

"It's how you see it. What really for me was a changing point was looking for the good that could come out of my bad situation. I purposely looked for it, and I molded that thing until I could see it—pitbull focus. And now, you know what? I'm living it."

~JAMILA DAVIS, AMERICAN AUTHOR, ACTIVIST AND FORMER FEDERAL PRISONER #59253-053

stone, slowly rubbing out the rough spots to reveal our natural brightness.

At all times the soul's calling is to receive. The soul does not choose what is good or bad. It does not say, "I will feel this, but not that." Or, "I will let you affect me, but I will not let you affect me." Just as our souls are durable, remaining alive and thriving wherever we are, they are also entirely permeable. These qualities come part and parcel. The more we let down our guard, the more we begin to see how deeply sensitive we are to everyone and everything. Where some people in the world may say that this sensitivity is weakness and our job is to become untouchable, the soul says that our sensitivity is our strength and our window into the interconnected reality of nature. The soul simply cannot fake it. You will experience this everywhere. You will walk into a room, and have an intuition of how your friends are feeling. You will sit down to eat, and immediately sense the tempo of the conversation already happening. Perhaps someone is emotionally charged, and the people are heavy and grave. Perhaps it is a more boisterous day, and jokes are being told and laughter is spilling off the table. This is your antennae, taking in information, informing you of your environment, and in this process you get changed. You are sensitive.

Our pain carries our greatest secrets. The greater the pain, the greater the secret.

Alchemy

An alchemist's job is to turn one material into another. We've all heard of the example, "turning lemons into lemonade." The other one is, "turning lead into gold." The alchemist doesn't avoid lemons, nor do they complain of having too much lead. The alchemist relies on both — the undesirable, often dismissed materials — because this is its base material for creating gold.

Base materials are where they do their life's work. We, too, can stop avoiding pain and actively seek it. When it's present, we seek to feel it. We reorient ourselves to sink further into relationship with it because we know the pain was brought to us to be converted to love. Feeling pain is knowing there is more humility to be gained and more of our made-up stories and false beliefs to strip away for a greater connection with God. It's said God will never give you more than you can handle.

You will experience a fundamental shift in your life where you no longer run from uncomfortable emotions or situations. You will grow the capacity to let go and relax in a world addicted to both material and spiritual achievement. You will allow yourself to sink in and feel rather than act out or have knee-jerk reactions. You will never again have to leave yourself.

We could call it healing, except we feel healing is too low of a goal. This process leaves you stronger. We believe this process of alchemy is the sole purpose of our lives and the fullest expression of our power. Everything we do is in service to this one single process, repeated over and over for the rest of our lives. We face what is in front of us, whether it be a backlog of emotion in our hearts or the accumulation of the injustice we face every day. Instead of fighting it or making it wrong or denying it, we admit it, we let it in and let it change us.

How we get where we're going determines what we get when we arrive. How you spend your time in prison determines who you are at the end of your time.

Like building a house — if you take care and use quality materials — the chances are better it will weather storms. If you take shortcuts or the foundation is shoddy, it's likely you will pay for it in the end, with interest. This house — your house — is your soul rearranging itself and reaching out beyond ideas of "good" and "bad" and into a world filled with richness of meaning.

An Alchemist's Greatest Tool

The answer to every prayer is approval; you are supposed to be here. Approval is synonymous with freedom; not giving in. "Accepting" life as it happens is the capacity to understand that this moment is right because you were presented with it. This moment and you were destined to meet. This moment is right; there is a natural intelligence at work. When you accept the moment, the intelligence goes to work for you. It is why we pray before we encounter difficulty: "God help me." You can replace this prayer with any prayer that works for you. We do this to help shoulder and face challenges we otherwise could not. We do not pray for the right circumstances to enter our lives, we pray for the power to face the circumstances we are in now. When Jamila Davis found herself facing 12 years for real estate fraud while working at Lehman Brothers, acceptance was the key to her freedom. She could no longer endlessly be bitter about the fact that she had landed in prison for doing the same thing many others got away with doing. Her high-flying career brokering real estate deals for hip hop artists and other celebrities was over, and in facing her new reality, she became a stronger and more powerful person than she ever was making deals in designer outfits in New York and New Jersey. This is the power of approval. How can I approve of what's happening right now? Can I love even this?

Approval is neutral, you are simply acknowledging what is and are willing to be with it because you know that being with something, without trying to change it, is how you harvest the benefit it is trying to offer you. Whatever life throws your way — pain, hurt, betrayal, regret, remorse — you can acknowledge it while staying firmly seated inside the house of your value.

Understand; approval is not endorsement. Approval is not saying difficult experiences are deserved or another person's poor behavior is acceptable. It's easy to confuse approval with endorsement, which is why people often disapprove of individuals, or even entire groups of people. It is as if we are so doggedly determined that something is wrong, we trick ourselves into refusing to see that it is happening. But of course, this is a strategy of a mind that remains stubbornly rooted in only acknowledging the reality it wants to see. The more mature mind sees that you can have approval for something without saying it's okay that it happened, and without liking it. You can approve of it, while not endorsing it. This isn't simply a choice of words, this is a choice that determines the story of your life. When you refuse to acknowledge something has happened, it rules you. When you acknowledge what has happened, you can then choose how you want to be with it.

Consider the story of Daryl Davis, a black author in the 1980s who interviewed the leader of a local KKK chapter, seeking to better understand his views. They continued correspondence and eventually a friendship grew. Daryl even attended KKK rallies led by the leader. After the events, they would embrace, even call each other friends. They did this for more than 10 years, though all the while the KKK leader stood firmly in his position that blacks were inferior.

Fifteen years into their friendship, the KKK leader came to his own natural conclusion: He'd been wrong. He denounced his position, retired his KKK robes, and began talking to others about the limitations of racism. Two hundred members of his KKK chapter left with him.

To simply disapprove of the KKK leader entirely, this friendship and ultimate transformation of the heart would never have occurred. It wasn't that Daryl endorsed racism, or endorsed the KKK. He never conceded to the KKK leader's points that he was inferior. Instead, he sought to understand the human being behind the undesirable actions. In doing so, he was able to turn hate into love, and ignorance into consciousness. No one was cast out, ostracized or shamed and future generations of these families will be forever changed.

What we hope you learn is a way to enact change by doing something other than being victimized or attacking or dominating or threatening a perpetrator into submission. That simply results in the same old loop; "victim" to "perpetrator" and back again. We hope you'll learn a deeper reconciliation with anyone or anything that had you locked out of your heart. By making friends with this pain, in this case racism, you begin to change the racist's mind. You begin their healing, and most importantly, yours.

Integration Exercises

- What was a painful experience I had as a child?

- What was a painful experience I have had as an adult?

- Do these experiences have anything in common? If so, what?

- What does forgiveness mean to me?

- Who do I refuse to forgive? Why?

- How do I benefit by not forgiving?

- Who do I refuse to love? Why?

- How do I benefit by not loving them?

- What part of living my life right now in prison do I feel will never be made right?

LESSON 3: EVERY VOICE INSIDE OF YOU IS TRYING TO HELP YOU

- How do I know this is true?

> *"If you bring forth what is within you, what you bring forth will save you. If you do not bring forth what is within you, what you do not bring forth will destroy you."*
>
> ~GOSPEL OF THOMAS

- Is it possible this is not true? How could that be possible?

- Aside from any crime, what is the biggest regret I carry?

"Until recently, I didn't express how I felt but I learned that the more I open up, the more I heal. When we forgive someone, there is a healthy balance of boundaries and internal peace as we grow and heal."

~Danielle, Central California Women's Facility

YOU WERE CHOSEN FOR FORGIVENESS

LESSON 4

Forgiveness is essential for a whole human life. It can come like a bolt from heaven or take decades of difficult work. Learning to forgive is an imperative for external as well as internal peace.

"The Choice"

In Iran, Samereh Alinejad suffered a mother's worst fear; her teenage son was stabbed to death by his friend Balal when the boys were just 18. From that day forward, rage and thoughts of revenge consumed her; little else was in her mind. Balal was caught, tried and sentenced to death. That country's penal code gives the victim's family a final say in capital punishment and she awaited the day she could take this man's life just as he had taken her son's. She longed for it, in fact.

In the months leading up to the execution, Samereh's dead son came to her in dreams asking that she spare his friend Balal. The dreams did nothing to soften her desire to see him dead.

In the last dream before the scheduled hanging, she dreamt her son would not speak to her. She didn't care.

"An eye for an eye," as the saying goes, is a fundamental part of Islamic justice, known as Sharia law, and on the day of the execution, her family dressed carefully and went to the prison. Balal's family did as well. As Balal was brought out to the gallows, something happened to Samereh.

"We must develop and maintain the capacity to forgive. He who is devoid of the power to forgive is devoid of the power to love. There is some good in the worst of us and some evil in the best of us."

~MARTIN LUTHER KING, JR.

In a flash of extreme genius, she forgave him. She had never given any indication she would, or even could, do so. Yet, as the noose went around his neck, perhaps she saw in his face the face of her son, a frightened young man doing the best he could in the face of chaos and violence. Perhaps a question ran through her mind, a terrible, terrible question. If she agreed to kill this man, what did that make her? Her extreme genius rose in this extreme situation in the most powerful way possible. She intuitively knew circles of violence and hatred don't stop until one side or the other steps up and forgives.

As Balal was released from the gallows, his mother reached through the fence to embrace Samereh in an emotional moment that transcended time and space. A photograph of them went around the world, offering hope to millions.

Samereh also forgave herself that day, too; she was free of her own hatred and thoughts of violence against this young man who had killed her son. Those thoughts disappeared in that moment of forgiveness. Samereh electrified the world, becoming a hero and symbol of the transformative nature of forgiveness. All of her beliefs and pretensions about justifiable punishment fell away when she refused to murder another soul, refused to take another child from another mother. She would not spend life searching for revenge; she chose love instead.

Your Calling Begins with Forgiveness

No one in power has ever been moved by coercion, shame or force, but rather they are moved naturally. People may change their actions based on being attacked, but real lasting change only occurs when their best efforts have been dignified, even when those best efforts fall short. Someone has to offer this acknowledgement first and model a new way. Your initiation into a world of profound inner peace is to become this person.

What Is Forgiveness?

Forgiveness is as simple as being willing to see the other person or yourself as human and allowing yourself to love them in the face of their mistake. Forgiveness is connecting to what someone's deeper, innocent motivations in acting a certain way are, even if acting this way caused you harm. It is opening to understanding that everyone is doing the best they can with the (often faulty) maps they were given. It is seeing that systems and institutions are made up of people who are all doing the best they can with their maps as well. It is not condoning terrible behavior or saying terrible harm is okay. It is connecting to the humanity of someone who caused harm — including you — and seeing, touching their innocence underneath it all.

What Happens When You Forgive

What you'll notice is people start to respond to you differently. All of us, yourself included, are looking for warm loving eyes to look back at us. God is as well. You can offer your warm gaze at a family picnic or inside a prison; that light is inside you no matter where you are.

Forgiveness changes everyone, beginning with you. Releasing the venom of hatred or resentment from your being fundamentally changes your capacity. What you previously forbade admission, you now have allowed in. You have followed the calling of your soul, which is to drop the judge's gavel of right and wrong, and instead to receive and to love.

There is no way to resent someone, or a group of people, as nasty or cruel, without seeing some part of that in you. Forgiveness grants mercy to the humanity of that other person or group of people, and in doing so grants mercy to yourself. You can now forgive yourself, too. There is no part of you, however deplorable, you ever have to dismiss again.

There is nothing the world needs more than people who rise to this challenge, who find the capability within themselves to answer this sacred call. It can seem like nothing you do from prison could have impact, but it can, and it does. When someone rises to forgive — society, their enemies, their friends, the system, themselves — they become a person who has freed themselves, regardless of all external conditions. A person like that has untold power, an immense positive impact on whoever they come into contact with. The energy ripples outward in ways you will never see.

There's a purpose to why you're here; it's the simple reason why anyone is anywhere. Your purpose happens to involve you being physically incarcerated inside of a prison, and the call on you is to ingest the darkness being bestowed upon you, and learn to transmute that darkness into love. People on the outside face their own set of unique hardships; they see the same faces of humanity that you do. The calling on their life is the same as yours. There is a purpose to everything.

Integration Exercises

Soulmaking – Your Genius

Our genius represents our deepest calling—it is the gifts we were endowed with to create in the world, and in doing so, be created ourselves. Experienced as "flow" or "effortlessness," it is that which emerges from us naturally. It is our essential selves.

WHAT WOULD YOU LIKE TO CULTIVATE IN THE FOLLOWING AREAS OF YOUR LIFE?

- Relationships & Connection With Others
  Example: I want to learn to share more vulnerably with other women. I want to make a friend where I know my friendship with her improves her life.

- Family
  Example: I want to write my daughter a letter every week.

- Personal Practices
  Example: I want to wake up early and do my morning practice every day before first count.

- Health
  Example: I want to have a doctor examine my leg and why it has been in pain.

- Faith & Spirit
  Example: I want to be a woman who relies on faith more than fighting.

- Community Contribution
  Example: I want to volunteer to contribute to the yard vegetable garden.

COMMITMENTS

This is where you commit. This agreement ultimately is with yourself. You have likely sensed or felt a new part of you emerging from this program and all of the hard work you have done. What do you commit to doing in order to continue this growth?

Example: I commit to doing Morning Practice everyday for 60 days. I commit to sharing one secret I have with a sister daily. I commit to letting my family know about this journey I am on. I commit to doing one helpful act for a staff member each day.

How to Support You

The final piece of this exercise lays out your "user's guide," the instruction manual to you. Consider the three most difficult to navigate behaviors you have, then write out how your friends and us can best handle them.

Example:

I will start my Morning Practice everyday and eventually grow "bored" and stop. When you notice me not doing practice, give me some attention and ask me if something is upsetting me. Usually I act "bored" when I am actually angry.

When you ask me how I am doing, I will say "I'm fine" even when I am not. This is me hiding. When you notice me hiding in this way, tell me a joke. Make me laugh. You can even make fun of me like saying "Oh, 'fine' huh? "Fed up, Insecure, Neurotic and Emotional?"

Thank You!

POST-PROGRAM ASSESSMENT AND QUESTIONNAIRE

Now that you have completed your journey, you will fill out the Human Flourishing Post-Assessment and the Post-Program Questionnaire.

You filled out the Human Flourishing Pre-Assessment at the beginning of the program as part of a measure of your overall fulfillment level. Now that you have completed the program, you will complete the Human Flourishing Post-Assessment.

You filled out The Pre-Program Questionnaire at the start of your program. Now that you have completed the program, you will fill out the Post-Program Questionnaire, again looking at your your emotions, thoughts, and actions.

The Human Flourishing Post-Program Assessment and the Post-Program Questionnaire are part of what you will mail or email back with your week seven assignment.

HUMAN FLOURISHING POST-ASSESSMENT

Name:

Select your level of agreement with each statement
(*only choose one answer*)

1. **In general, I feel confident and positive about myself.**

   STRONGLY AGREE   AGREE   UNDECIDED

   DISAGREE   STRONGLY DISAGREE

2. **I made some mistakes in the past, but I feel that all in all everything has worked out for the best.**

   STRONGLY AGREE   AGREE   UNDECIDED

   DISAGREE   STRONGLY DISAGREE

3. **Many days I wake up feeling discouraged about how I have lived my life.**

   STRONGLY AGREE   AGREE   UNDECIDED

   DISAGREE   STRONGLY DISAGREE

4. **My relationships are as satisfying as I would want them to be.**

   STRONGLY AGREE   AGREE   UNDECIDED

   DISAGREE   STRONGLY DISAGREE

5. **I believe I have discovered who I really am.**

   STRONGLY AGREE   AGREE   UNDECIDED

   DISAGREE   STRONGLY DISAGREE

6. **My life is centered around a set of core beliefs that give meaning to my life.**

   STRONGLY AGREE   AGREE   UNDECIDED

   DISAGREE   STRONGLY DISAGREE

7. **I can say that I have found my purpose in life.**

   STRONGLY AGREE   AGREE   UNDECIDED

   DISAGREE   STRONGLY DISAGREE

8. **I believe I know what I was meant to do in life.**

   STRONGLY AGREE   AGREE   UNDECIDED

   DISAGREE   STRONGLY DISAGREE

9. **I have confidence in my opinions, even if they are contrary to the general consensus.**

   STRONGLY AGREE   AGREE   UNDECIDED

   DISAGREE   STRONGLY DISAGREE

10. **I usually know what I should do because some actions just feel right to me.**

    STRONGLY AGREE   AGREE   UNDECIDED

    DISAGREE   STRONGLY DISAGREE

11. **I find I get intensely involved in many of the things I do each day.**

    STRONGLY AGREE   AGREE   UNDECIDED

    DISAGREE   STRONGLY DISAGREE

12. **I feel best when I'm doing something worth investing a great deal of effort in.**

   STRONGLY AGREE   AGREE   UNDECIDED

   DISAGREE   STRONGLY DISAGREE

13. **When I engage in activities that involve my best potentials, I have this sense of really being alive.**

   STRONGLY AGREE   AGREE   UNDECIDED

   DISAGREE   STRONGLY DISAGREE

Post-Program Questionnaire

Name:

Select your level of agreement with each statement
(*only choose one answer*)

1. **Since starting this course, on a scale of 1-10,** (1 being the lowest and 10 being the highest) **please circle below how much stress you feel on a day-to-day basis?**

   1   2   3   4   5   6   7   8   9   10

2. **Since starting this course, on a scale of 1-10,** (1 being the lowest and 10 being the highest) **please circle below how angry you feel on a day-to-day basis?**

   1   2   3   4   5   6   7   8   9   10

3. **Since starting this course, on a scale of 1-10,** (1 being the lowest and 10 being the highest) **please circle below how optimistic you are about your life?**

   1   2   3   4   5   6   7   8   9   10

4. **Since starting this course, on a scale of 1-10,** (1 being the lowest and 10 being the highest) **how significant a role do drugs, alcohol, or other substances play in your life?**

   1   2   3   4   5   6   7   8   9   10

5. **Since starting this course, how frequently did you get into physical fights?** (Please circle your answer below.)

   NEVER   INFREQUENTLY   SOMETIMES

   SOMEWHAT OFTEN   OFTEN

6. **Since starting this course, how frequently did you get into verbal fights?** (Please circle your answer below.)

   NEVER   INFREQUENTLY   SOMETIMES

   SOMEWHAT OFTEN   OFTEN

7. **Since starting this course, have you felt depressed?** (Please circle your answer below.)

   NEVER   INFREQUENTLY   SOMETIMES

   SOMEWHAT OFTEN   OFTEN

8. **Since starting this course, have you had suicidal thoughts?** (Please circle your answer below.)

   NEVER   INFREQUENTLY   SOMETIMES

   SOMEWHAT OFTEN   OFTEN

9. **Since starting this course, how often did you feel grateful for your life?** (Please circle your answer below.)

   NEVER   INFREQUENTLY   SOMETIMES

   SOMEWHAT OFTEN   OFTEN

10. **Describe your experience of the course. What did you like? What didn't you like? What did you learn?**

11. Have you noticed any changes in your life? Please share anything you'd like us to know.

12. Are there limiting beliefs you used to carry about your life which you no longer believe are true? If yes, what were those beliefs and how have they changed?

13. Have you noticed any changes in your relationships? If yes, please describe them.

14. Do you feel more forgiving of yourself as a result of this course?

15. How has the daily routine (yoga, Daily Soul Letters, meditation) impacted you? Please be specific.

16. Do you feel any differently about the purpose of your time spent incarcerated?

17. What do you believe about the statement "you can live free inside of prison"?

18. What could we do to improve this course?

19. We would love to hear anything else you would like us to know about your experience of the course! Please share your thoughts below.

SHARE YOUR EXPERIENCE

Restoring basic dignity means that we are restoring the idea that every single human being, no matter what happened in their life, has a purpose. You have the capacity to convert your life's pain into a meaningful contribution. You have an impact greater than you may know.

Monastic living inside of a prison is the ultimate form of converting poison into medicine. This process of alchemy can continue for you by sharing what you experienced. We want to offer you the ability to use your experiences with *The Art of Soulmaking* to create a narrative about the power of this process. Your experience can not only encourage others to pick up the tools you chose to pick up, but it can support and help them make sense of the experiences they are having as they journey forward.

Your story will change the world outside the walls, too. Many people in the free world, outside the walls, attempt to make this journey and fail. The distractions are endless. If you made it, you have something to offer anyone, regardless of whether they are incarcerated or not.

To participate in co-creating this narrative, please read and sign the **Writing Release Form**.

If you need more space to write about your experience than what is provided on the Writing Release Form, you can submit additional pages along with your signed release form. Share your experience with us electronically, or using the mailing address below:

Unconditional Freedom Project
PO Box 305
Newark, CA 94560

WRITING RELEASE FORM

The **Unconditional Freedom Project** at times uses writings from participants like you to promote the program to current and potential participants and supporters. If you'd like to share anything, please click the box here "Accept" which indicates that you understand and release rights to the writing in this box.

By checking the box, "Accept," I, _____, hereby grant Unconditional Freedom Project (an initiative of Unconditional Freedom, a California non-profit) (UFP) and their partners, who help publicize their programming, permission to copy, exhibit, publish or distribute what I have written on this page. I verify that what I have written is my original creation. I understand that at no time shall I be paid, compensated or given royalties, now or at any point in the future by UFP. I hereby irrevocably authorize UFP and its partners who help publicize the program to copy, exhibit, publish or distribute my content. I also give the right for UFP to make any edits they deem necessary to publish my content. I understand that UFP does not guarantee publication of my released materials.

☐ Accept

Share any thing about your experience here:

WRITING RELEASE FORM

_____
_____
_____
_____
_____
_____
_____
_____
_____
_____
_____
_____
_____
_____
_____
_____
_____
_____
_____
_____

I understand that if I don't indicate how I wish to be referred to on the line below, I authorize UFP to use my first name and last initial in association with my written work.

Name to publish with my writings (please print):

_____

Signature: _____

Date: _____

SOULMAKING COMMUNITY

Even though you've graduated from the *Art of Soulmaking* course, this path to living a monastic life continues on. You start to see daily life through a different lens, and engage with your interior world in new ways. Many of us have been working with this material for years and find new insights each day, finding that over time we deepen the experience of our lives. Soulmaking is a lifelong journey.

We created the Soulmaking Community because we recognize that you cannot make a soul alone. The desire to feel seen and felt by another is what makes us human. Not only is it natural, it is medicine. Soulmaking Groups offer an opportunity to deepen your journey and foster connections along the way.

For those who feel called to lead these group meetings, your experience in alchemizing difficult experiences and emotions, your wrestle with a higher power of your understanding, your struggles with forgiveness all become a rallying point around which others can make their way on this path. You organize, you encourage, you live as an example; not of perfection but of what's possible when you embrace being human.

For those attending these group meetings, your willingness to share your thoughts, insights from your practices, your emotions, your pain, your victories — this is how you become more you. You integrate everything you find within yourself on this path, and this inspires others to do the same.

There is also something essential about seeing others. Seeing their humanity allows us to see our own. Sometimes our own humanity is too difficult to look at directly but if we can see it in another, we can see it in ourselves.

We discover ourselves in our own eyes, and in the eyes of others; we discover that we are both unique, and in many ways the same as others. We realize that what we think makes us difficult, wrong or bad is what makes us human and relatable. We can only come to find these truths through connection and sharing, and that is what lies at the heart of our Soulmaking Groups.

Group facilitators will be provided meeting scripts that encourage interactive discussion on the following topics:

- Soul Letters
- Meditation
- Yoga
- Basic Goodness
- Victim Consciousness
- Alchemy
- Forgiveness
- Soulmaker Movement Principles

If you're interested in becoming a Soulmaking Group Facilitator, fill out the application on the next page and submit it to the mailing address below or electronically.

We look forward to working with you!

Unconditional Freedom Project
PO Box 305
Newark, CA 94560

SOULMAKING GROUP FACILITATOR APPLICATION

---

1. What called me to become a Soulmaking Community leader?

2. What are the gifts I would offer to another in the program?

3. What are the gifts I would receive by stepping into this position?

4. What words of encouragement would I have wanted to hear going into this program, that I can now pass on to another?

5. What do I envision for this community I'm helping create?

ADDITIONAL LETTERS TO THE NEWCOMER

To those considering The Art of Soulmaking:

Last year, I unexpectedly received The Art of Soulmaking *in the mail. I read the introduction and was hooked. I got right to work that evening. Since that night, the program has greatly improved my life in prison and has provided me with tools that will continue to benefit me long after my release.*

One of the first benefits I noticed was the structure and purpose the daily practices added to my mornings, when prison life feels especially slow and listless for me. Instead, I wake up, get a glass of water, work through my daily practices, and go about my day.

Each practice has become a fulfilling part of my days. My days feel incomplete without them now. The yoga is refreshing and relaxing. The meditation declutters the mind and helps me work through problems. The Soul Letters are cathartic, therapeutic, and insightful. I've found I now fixate on the negative less and my days pass more quickly.

Perhaps the most rewarding part of the workbook has been how it's encouraged and helped me to reimagine and reflect on how I can transform my time and suffering into something greater and beneficial to me and those around me. I've learned that my environment doesn't dictate my life or define who I am in this world. The program has helped me to actively practice contemplation and self-examination.

When I first began The Art of Soulmaking *program, I encountered puzzled looks and questions as I did my daily practices. At first, I was a little self-conscious but this quickly passed. People got used to my* routine and some even grew interested in completing the program themselves.

Many of us in prison are seeking meaningful ways to improve our lives and form healthy routines, so sharing these ideas and tools has been another rewarding aspect of the experience. As you work through this program, I encourage you to share your experiences and workbook with your peers.

It's been said the hardest part of a journey is taking the first step. Now that The Art of Soulmaking *is in your hands, I hope you'll do what I did and commit to following through with this course to its completion and giving its message and practices an honest try. I'm writing this nearly a year after beginning my journey and I'm incredibly thankful I happened across this program and gave it a shot.*

It's my hope that anyone who may read this, chooses to utilize The Art of Soulmaking, *and use their time to better themselves in ways that will persist far beyond the prison's walls and razor wire.*

Best Wishes,
Thom

Thomas is currently incarcerated in Virginia. He discovered *The Art of Soulmaking* while in prison at the age of twenty-nine.

To The Art of Soulmaking *newcomer, I began reading* The Art of Soulmaking *and participating in the AoS program as a result of my exploration in mindfulness. Over the past few years, my focus has been on mindful communication. I was exploring possibilities on how to manifest mindful communication into action (challenging my old thought and verbal patterns). I stumbled into this program. I read through the AoS workbook and was invigorated by the contents. The Soulmaker Principles in the workbook articulated concepts and ideas that had previously been only vague wisps of thought and intentions.*

Participating in this program has solidified my opinion that true change comes through pausing and connecting with each other on a human-to-human level. Our emotions, our thoughts, and our actions are similar regardless of where we come from or where we find ourselves in our present moment. When I think about what is needed to create human flourishing in our world, the answer always points back to connection, to fostering that understanding of shared humanity and interrelated welfare. To seeing beyond the labels put upon us, and opening the doors to the possibility of a new world that has space and understanding for all our lived experiences.

Learning how to see and live **truth** *is a challenging pathway. The workbook offers tools to see situations with a little more clarity. Having letters with our penpals and meeting with other volunteers has been valuable in supporting my own efforts of internal reflection and transmutation. We come together to create community, support, and grace for the effort it takes to transform those aspects of ourselves that no longer serve us. It is helpful to converse with others who are also on the path of introspection and transformation of their pain into something greater than themselves. Participating in the Unconditional Freedom project has given me the opportunity to make connections with folks I might not otherwise have met. I have received a lot of wisdom I am able to put into practice in my own daily living.*

There are many days I am distraught about the state of the world I find myself living in. The increased levels of violence against each other interpersonally, nationally, and globally are overwhelming. I see my participation with this group as an opportunity to put my values into action. I do this in an effort to serve humanity. To serve love, kindness, establish understanding with some who may have had a different life experience than I have had. In having conversations that enrich my mind and my soul, I am healed as much as I hope to offer healing. I am comforted as much as I hope to comfort. Knowing someone sees you, listens to you, and actually cares about you can have a deeply profound effect on a person's heart. If my heart can be softened and your heart can be softened, then the world is that much softer for everyone else.

Too often our society shuns those who are "others," and at a great loss. So often the perpetrators are victims themselves as a result of years of intergenerational violence and trauma. It is my opinion that the way to stop the cycle of violence and "othering" is to pause and connect with each other for conversations and to understand that when I hurt you, I am hurting myself. I hope by having these talks we'll develop more understanding of ourselves and each other as fellow humans and work together to put more loving energy out into the universe. I want to love as many people as I possibly can in this world. I believe we are all one. I am hopeful that sharing my experience may motivate others to participate in this uplifting work.

Signed,
Mary

Mary Stockwell-White has been studying *The Art of Soulmaking* for close to two years. She currently volunteers as a letter writer for Unconditional Freedom's *Art of Soulmaking* Prison penpal program, through which she exchanges letters with individuals who are incarcerated and are also studying the workbook.

FROM THE AUTHORS

Beth Wareham: I am a longtime writer and editor with an extensive list of books behind me. I have written three of my own—two nonfiction and one novel—and have ghostwritten countless others.

I pride myself on being a generalist, allowing for maximum learning as I go through life. I spent the majority of my career as a publisher at Simon and Schuster. An adventuress, I have tracked elephants on foot in Zimbabwe, kayaked with Right whales in the Bay of Fundy, and ridden across the Pampas of Chile. After I lost half of my family in a six-week period, my travels turned more inward. I stepped back from life for a year of what I can only call mourning, the first step in a long process of rebuilding my internal world after that trauma. I live in New York City with my husband and two cats, Carmelo and LaLa.

Nicole Daedone: I want to know life biblically, the way a man knows a woman, the way a lover knows a beloved. I want to know the water by getting wet. Theory, commandments, concepts leave me hollow. My driving questions when I come across dicta and dogma are, Is that true? Is it wholly true? Where and how is it true? For whom is it true and why? Can it withstand the test of time? Is it true for me as a woman? The last one has taken me off many a beaten path. Givens are often no longer givens when I ask this question. The world turns upside down. As a free woman, I want all things to be free, liberated from any ideas I would impose on them.

We are constructed of the divine. I believe everything—and I mean everything—when properly tended to, reveals an untold beauty. But my work is not as activist, reformer, saint, teacher, guru, or shaman—it is as artist. The art I do is akin to found-object art: art made from what has been thrown away. It's an art that turns something back into itself. Like turning prisons into monasteries; the degradation of addiction into the art of addiction that isolates the addiction drive for purposes of realization; the life sentence of trauma into human flourishing; the feminism of subjugated women into the feminine collective of inestimable power; those who have been canceled, exiled, and banished into the leaders of the next era; desertified soil into not only carbon-absorbing but nutrient-producing; hunger and food deserts into farm-to-table, free, pop-up restaurants; black culture into the black box for society that holds the secrets. These programs exist, and you can find them here: www.unconditionalfreedom.org.

My work remains as it always was: to turn poison into medicine and make it available to those who want it. But for those who need it, here is the conventional side of things: I graduated from San Francisco State University with a degree in semantics and gender communication. I cofounded the popular avant-garde art gallery, 111 Minna Gallery, in San Francisco's SoMa. I have appeared on *ABC News Nightline*, and my work has been featured in *The New York Times, New York Post, San Francisco Chronicle*, and *7x7 Magazine*, among others. I've written for *Tricycle: The Buddhist Review*.

Made in the USA
Middletown, DE
24 August 2024

59138647R00075